ASPECTS OF MODERN SOCIOLOGY

General Editors

John Mays Emeritus Professor of Sociology, University of Liverpool
Maurice Craft Professor of Education, University of Nottingham

This Longman library of texts in modern sociology consists of three Series, and includes the following titles:

THE SOCIAL STRUCTURE OF MODERN BRITAIN

The family
Mary Farmer
formerly University of
Liverpool

Population
Prof. R. K. Kelsall
formerly University of
Sheffield

The welfare state
Prof. David Marsh
formerly University of
Nottingham

**Structures and processes of
Urban life**
Prof. R. E. Pahl
University of Kent
R. Flynn
University of Salford
N. H. Buck
University of Kent

The middle class
Prof. John Raynor
The Open University
and
Roger King
Huddersfield Polytechnic

Leisure
Kenneth Roberts
University of Liverpool

The mass media
Peter Golding
University of Leicester

The economic structure
Prof. Cedric Sandford
University of Bath

Migration

J. A. JACKSON, BA (Hiram, Ohio) MA (Lond., Dubl.),
Professor and Head of Department of Sociology,
Trinity College, Dublin

Longman London and New York

Longman Group Limited
Longman House, Burnt Mill, Harlow
Essex CM20 2JE, England
Associated companies throughout the world

*Published in the United States of America
by Longman Inc., New York*

First published 1986

British Library Cataloguing in Publication Data

Jackson, J.A.
    Migration.—(Aspects of modern sociology.
    Social processes)
    1. Emigration and immigration
    I. Title   II. Series
    304.8   JV6021

ISBN 0-582-48052-3

Library of Congress Cataloging-in-Publication Data
Migration.
    (Aspects of modern sociology. Social processes)
    Bibliography: p.
    Includes inindex
    1. Migration, Internal—Great Britain.   2. Labor
mobility—Great Britain.   3. Social change.   I. Jackon,
J.A. (John Archer), 1929-   . II. Series.
HB2043.M54   1986   304.8′0941   85-13098
ISBN 0-582-48052-3

COL B 0715/5.95 3.90

Produced by Longman Singapore Publishers (Pte) Ltd.
Printed in Singapore.

CONTENTS

EDITORS' PREFACE

The first series in Longman's *Aspects of Modern Sociology* library was concerned with the social structure of modern Britain, and was intended for students following professional and other courses in universities, polytechnics, colleges of education, and elsewhere in further and higher education, as well as for those members of a wider public wishing to pursue an interest in the nature and structure of British society.

A further series set out to examine the history, aims, techniques and limitations of social research; and this third series is concerned with a number of fundamental social processes. The presentation in each case is basically analytical, but each title will also seek to embody a particular viewpoint. It is hoped that these very relevant introductory texts will also prove to be of interest to a wider, lay readership as well as to students in higher education

John Barron Mays
Maurice Craft

FOREWORD

This book represents a remarkable act of faith on the part of the editors and publishers of the series and I am grateful for the patience and indulgence shown to a somewhat wayward and tardy author.

Migration remains one of the key factors in the process of social change and development and for this reason it opens up fascinating avenues of social enquiry and because of a tendency to think holistically about societies, of theory also. A brief book can merely sketch a few of the dimensions and hopefully whet the appetite for those who take the interchange of population as an exciting challenge in the development of plural society.

My debts are many. Most of all to Dee Jones whose typing converted a scrawl into defensible statement. Martha Lyons drew an excellent sketch map and several graduate students of the Department of Sociology helped at different stages with bibliographical checking. Needless to say, even for a short book my family put up with a lot and remained unfailingly supportive. Authorship, like migration, is a high-risk activity involving a degree of exposure that it is hard to manage alone. I am grateful to all those who have helped the process though the product clearly remains my responsibility and not theirs.

J. A. Jackson

ACKNOWLEDGEMENTS

We are indebted to the following for permission to reproduce copyright material:

Routledge & Kegan Paul for an extract and a map from pp. 70, 12 *The Irish in Britain* by J. A. Jackson (1963); United Nations Educational, Scientific and Cultural Organization for an extract and two maps from pp. 7, 31, 34 *Study on the Dynamics, Evolution and Consequences of Migration II: Three Centuries of Spatial Mobility in France* (c) Unesco 1983.

1

MIGRATION AS A SOCIAL PROCESS

Introduction

Human societies are not static and have generally been subject to
disasters, wars and traumas which have caused migration, eviction
and the search for refuge. Societies in any case are varied in their
stability or mobility. In some instances extremely sedentary
economic and social relations have ensured situations where people
could predictably expect to be born, to live and to die under the
same roof. In other situations regular flows of migration have
provided a stable and predictable pattern linked to the seasons or to
annual migrations of domesticated or wild herds of animals, birds
or fish. Such migrations are also undertaken for the harvest of
seasonal crops or in recognition of seasonal changes in farming
patterns such as transhumance. In the main they are patterned,
regular and to be distinguished from violent upheavals of one kind
or another.

All such movements are pre-eminently social in character. They
are indications of a change in status that is manifested by a change
in spatial relationships. Even at a microscopic level this tends to be
true. Within the home, changes in status from baby to child, or
from adolescent to adult, are all accompanied by changes in
physical relationship. Certain chairs, parts of the house or parts of
the room or the farmyard or garden are reserved for the specific use
of those performing roles associated with age and status. Such
changes are signified and symbolized by a transition of property or
object relations.

Clearly these changes are most significant when the individual
moves to an entirely new social and physical environment. Charac-

teristically we think of migrants changing house and establishing a new dwelling place, usually a change of work location is involved together with a breakaway from old social ties and the forging of new ones. With modern transport it is possible for considerable distances to be maintained between house and work so that these boundaries are not conterminous and a change in one does not necessarily imply a change in the other. At the extremes are those whose work itself is migratory – oil men, gangers, soldiers, sailors. Particularly when unmarried, they rather like a snail carry their homes with them, having no regular domestic space apart from that provided by the work situation they are in.

However it comes about, migration raises particular and challenging analytical difficulties for the demographer, sociologist or economist who conventionally uses one society as the boundary for analysis. Migration implies movement of individuals and groups between two societies; that which they have left and that to which they have come. The process is usually achieved by physical movement and consequent change of residence and other circumstance. It is no different in character to the transitions that are achieved as the result of slow or sharp historical movements that bring about a radical change in circumstance for those who have lived through them. Such processes involve a paradigm shift which makes it difficult if not impossible to go back to the old ways, to accept a world without electricity or the pre-Galilean concept of the universe. Therefore it is necessary when discussing this social process to keep in mind the large as well as the small dimension. Although migration is expressed through the actual movement of individuals from A to B, that movement contrasts and compares two whole societies which continue to exist in encapsulated form in the migrant individual whose experience straddles and to an extent reconciles each to the other.

A prevailing and pervading feature in the study of migration has been the myth of the static society. The assumption, more or less clearly expressed, that the natural condition of man is sedentary has been responsible for a number of misconceptions regarding the nature of migration. In some ways this is associated with the fact that migration is correctly perceived as an agent of change in that it implies a threat posed by the migrant to the stability of a form of social organization that is complete and comprehensive of all its members. In contrast to industrial societies the pre-industrial society has been depicted as static, in spite of the mass of evidence of movement in medieval Europe, let alone the great caravans of migrants moving across Asia and Africa and the Mediterranean basin from earliest times.

A contributing feature of this static model has been the adoption of a holistic functionalist model of society which has, inevitably, left the migrant to be depicted as an outsider, or marginal person, a deviant in relation to the settled society. It would be wrong to make too much of this point but the reality is that migration is not a new phenomenon associated with industrial society. It does of course take a different form in such a society, since the means of transport have changed and distances that formerly took weeks and months can now be covered in days and hours by train and plane. Beyond that though, the process of migration remains essentially similar involving decisions and opportunities in all societies that were dependent on movement for at least some of the population in every community. If they were not driven to leave then others, 'outsiders', might arrive in a constant ebb and flow of conquest, trade and restless search for human and material wealth.

The historian Fernand Braudel most eloquently captures the spirit of dynamic movement in his reconstruction of the society that bordered the Mediterranean in the fifteenth and sixteenth centuries.[1] Neither mountains nor sea tended to condition stability and deserts were passage routes in much the same way as the sea surrounded by ports and islands of settled habitation. The settled populations of the valleys and lowland plains were if anything atypical of the restless mass of humanity that flowed through and around their communities. Indeed as in later centuries, emigration from the mountains and across the seas was essential to the development of the towns and cities of Europe, let alone to the development of the conquests and colonial expansion that characterized the development of monarchical ambitions and the aggrandizement of both city and nation states.

Equally the movement may come about gradually or be remarkably sudden and traumatic. The dispersal of children from the family 'nest' is an anticipated and necessary process of the transition to adulthood and the achievement of independence. Such movement allows the steady continuity of social relations reproduced within the framework of the known world. There will certainly be an emotional wrench to mark the transition but there is nothing unexpected about it. In the case of capture or eviction or flight there is no time to prepare for the event and get used to the idea. Similarly in cases of marital breakdown relocation by one or both partners becomes a necessary outcome of the changing social relationship that forced the household and its members apart.

Here we are talking of a series of changing social relationships and roles that are at one time or another the experience of everyone. Few people in contemporary industrialized societies are born and die in the same house, particularly when both these processes are institutionalized in hospital and involve temporary migrations at both the beginning and the end of life. How can we distinguish migration in a meaningful way from the ebb and flow of normal social experience? We will in the next section of this chapter deal more formally with concepts and definitions but for the moment we can define some initial guidelines.

First, we will expect a migration to be a *significant* movement. By this we mean that it has demographic consequences such that the move has involved a shift across a definite administrative boundary. This will of course mean that we will not consider as migration moving Grandad into a 'granny flat' in the same village or small town, so some quite significant moves will be missed out. However, every move to another town or across a county or district line we will include as migration.

Second, migration must be sustained. In other words the movement is not temporary or casual. A holiday is not migration, nor is a temporary visit on business.

Third, migration must involve a distinct social transition involving a change of status or a changed relationship to the social as well as the physical environment.

These three guidelines will be useful in considering the problems posed by both the available concepts and the available data by which we can establish whether or not migration has taken place. It should be borne in mind that they are only guidelines which depend on the theoretical and methodological assumptions that we bring to the question. They underline the three domains: spatial, temporal and social, which any theory or method that deals with the process of migration must take into consideration.

Notes and definitions

I want in this section to try and set out some basic features and definitions of the migration process; these will be discussed and refined further in the course of the chapters that follow but they should provide some initial indicators to help us outline the rather complex social process that we are discussing. Part of its complexity arises from the fact that migration is a matter studied by a number of different disciplines – demography, economics, sociology, geography, etc. – each of which tends to place its own gloss on the topic.

1. *Migration*. The movement, temporarily or permanently, from one physical location to another of a population.

(*a*) Temporary migration implies that the place of permanent residence is maintained while the migrant is away for a period of work in another country or another part of the country. Such migration may occur on a regular or seasonal basis as with transhumance or harvest migration or migration with flocks or herds of reindeer;

(*b*) Permanent migration implies a clear change of residence based on a decision to move. Clearly there may be some indeterminacy between these two categories and in many instances temporary migrants may end up as permanent.

2. *Periodization*. Migration is usually measured over a specific period of time in order to assess its effect. Often this may be governed by other population interests such as the dates of the decennial census. The extent of change in a population between two periods is a product of a combination of three factors, birth rate, death rate and migration. The migration so measured is always the *net migration*, since it constitutes the *net* effect of migration only and does not record the number of moves that have taken place but have been cancelled out by counter-moves, nor temporary or seasonal moves that have taken place within the period in question.

3. *Immigration*. This term is used to describe the process of entry into a country or within it to a different administrative district. The extent to which this process is formalized varies. In some countries, such as Norway and Sweden, every change of residence must be reported to the police and other authorities and

forms part of the continuous registration process. In others such as Britain or the United States there are no formal registration mechanisms for internal migrants apart from electoral registers, but changes may be indicated by factors associated with residential change such as changes in contracts for domestic services such as telephone and electricity.

International immigration tends to be formalized with border controls at entry and distinctions between categories of entrant made in terms of the willingness of the country in question to give permanent, temporary or visitor status to different types of migrant. Migrants may be excluded because of lack of skills, age, nationality, race, health, lack of funds, or for criminal or ideological reasons. The result of these formal mechanisms is that relatively full statistical data are produced indicating the characteristics of the immigrant population that is admitted.

4. *Emigration*. This term covers movement away from a residential location either within the same country or to another country. For the reasons given under immigration above there are often no official records of this process as such within the country. The same in general is true of those who emigrate to another country and most countries do not keep established records of the number of their nationals who are living·in another country. Some information may, however, be available for specific administrative purposes such as taxation. Certain categories of emigrant remain in contact with their country of origin through their embassy in the country of residence. These, however, tend to be a minority and figures held by embassies tend to underrepresent the emigrant population to a substantial degree.

5. *Birthplace*. Migration data is often drawn from census data gathered in response to a question on place of birth. This usually covers town and administrative district for those born within the country and country for those born elsewhere. Occasionally this is linked to a change of residence question as in the 1961 UK Census which asked people to indicate where they were living ten years ago. Usually no periodic distinction is made and consequently the birthplace information is subject to age bias in the response as well as having the further disadvantages referred to earlier that place of birth and previous nationality or administrative area may not be consistent.

Thus a person may have never moved from the house in which he was born and still be recorded as a migrant if there has been a change in administrative boundary in the meantime. It should be noted that birthplace data only describes the respondents' generation. It excludes children of immigrants and other relatives who have been born in the receiving country, for instance the children of a Pakistani, Irish or German family in the United Kingdom, nor does it take account of other migrations during the intervening period.

6. *Accommodation and assimilation*. These two terms are linked and describe the process whereby immigrants become established in a new location. The immigrant as a new Australian or new Briton will meet with varying degrees of acceptance and will gradually learn the requirements of living in the new environment, learning a new language and adapting to different customs and practices. It is a highly complex process which we will be examining in detail later in the book. It will vary if the migration is of long or short duration, as will the provision of official aids and schemes to help the immigrant make the necessary adjustments. Clearly the whole question is coloured by the attitude of the immigrant himself and the society to which he has come at both an informal and a formal level.

7. *Voluntary migration*. This term covers any move in which the decision to migrate is entered into as a free alternative available to the individual. Clearly that decision may be subject to many influences and factors in the individual's 'market situation' but it is not formally constrained.

8. *Forced migration*. Such migrations involve moves of necessity for the protection of life and liberty of individuals. They may be political refugees such as the Vietnamese boat people or Hungarians after the 1956 rising. In all cases they are people who are imperilled by remaining where they are, in their own judgement or that of others. The extent to which their exile is regarded as legitimate by potential receiving countries varies and conditions their admission as immigrants and may vary between those who are specifically considered to be political or religious exiles and those who are avoiding penalties for criminal offences or escaping taxation penalties in their home country.

9. *Internal migration*. This term involves moves within a country

or prescribed area; normally it does not involve formal controls at border points but it does imply movement across administrative boundaries.

10. *International migration.* This movement involves individuals or families moving across national boundaries to establish themselves in a different country. Migration always implies change of residence. Such migrations normally involve changing place of employment but this does not follow in the case of some of those living near boundaries who may be able to commute daily to their place of work in the original country of residence.

11. *Return migration.* This involves a return and resettlement of a migrant population in their original country or area of residence. Such returns may occur quite soon after the original move or occur at specific stages in the life cycle such as the retirement stage.

These notes and definitions do not comprehend all of the detailed and specific issues that we shall be dealing with in the chapters which follow. They form an initial listing to clarify the dimensions of the problems of definition.

Migration data

One of the major limiting factors in the conceptual analysis of migration flows and patterns is the capacity that we have to measure movement. In general those studying migration have had to rely on such official published statistics that are available as the source of their data and this conditions their capacity to analyse the process, even in terms of the quantitative effects that migration has within the framework of population studies.

Three components account for change in population. These are births, deaths and migration. Thus in order to estimate the size of a given population five years later we would need to know the number of births and the number of deaths that we could expect in the period, together with the extent of inward and outward migration. Thus it should be possible using the census results together with the annual reports of birth and death data to make a precise calculation of population change. However, there are a number of difficulties to be overcome depending on the purpose of the enquiry. Some of them will be immediately obvious and arise from the fact that both census data and the Registrar-General's reports are aggregated over quite large populations and may not adequately distinguish differences that affect part of the population under review, or age structure, or age of marriage, all of which may affect the extent of population change differentially as between immigrants and native population.

The limitations of the data available for migration studies start with the census. Although official estimates of populations exist from earliest times it is not until the nineteenth century that most European countries developed a systematic method of enumerating the population and publishing the results in a generally accessible form. The basic units in which it is published are by country and by county. The first is the basis for the analysis of international migration and the second internal migration. Immediate problems arise, however, when the geographical boundaries of either are altered and comparisons between different census periods may have to take account of changes in boundaries which have arisen over time. The county as an administrative unit in the UK for instance is an amalgam of ancient counties, administrative counties and local government districts with different administrative functions such as health, welfare and registration corresponding to each. (These difficulties are well documented by Baines.[2]) It is therefore necessary when making a statistical analysis of variation over a long period to take a 'standard' unit of measurement which can be maintained by appropriate adjustment throughout the period of study. Similar difficulties obviously exist in making analyses of international migration and again it is necessary to pay particular attention to the administrative requirement of the census itself. If it is primarily for national administrative functions it may not appear necessary to include temporary migrant workers or other non-nationals, since these in a literal sense 'do not count'. Thus in looking at the migration statistics of Romania in the late 1960s, at a period when there was popularly known to be a significant loss of Romanian population travelling to Austria, there was no official recognition of this fact in the published statistics. On being asked how such outmigrants were recorded I was told that they were for official purposes recorded as dead.

Census data is also limited with regard to the amount of detail that is given. Counties of birthplace are given for the UK from 1851 onwards but again variations exist largely because the concept of place by which people subjectively operate may not correspond precisely to the actual administrative county within which they reside. For example people may define themselves as Londoners although they live in Middlesex, or Welsh even though they live in Monmouthshire. Those with birthplaces in Scotland or Ireland were always recorded without the specific county being listed in censuses in the UK. Similarly English or Scots resident in Ireland would only be listed by country rather than county when enumerated there.

These difficulties all arise from the fact that the census, while a most valuable source for statistical analysis, is constructed primarily with objectives that reflect the predominant administrative concerns of the state and the political process at any particular time. Similar consequences occur from the lack of standardization of immigration legislation and variations in control and consequently record of entry or exit of persons.

It will also be apparent that the analysis of intercensual change depends on the consistency of collection of variables that can be associated with the migration process. In some cases nationality may be substituted for birthplace so that only aliens are recorded as immigrants, age and sex may not be distinguished and so on.

These problems with the census volumes as a source point up the fact that much of the migration data available to researchers must be extracted in a raw form and has not been subjected to any initial analysis by the Census Office. This is certainly the case in the UK until recent years in contrast to the situation in the US or other countries where migration has been given particular political salience in relation to immigration patterns and ethnic and minority interests. This varying emphasis, which accounts for the adequacy of character of the data at different periods, also varies between different national governments and produces different emphases and interest among those undertaking research.

In addition to census volumes a certain amount of information on migration patterns is available from labour and manpower statistics and can be deduced by changes in administrative records of the social security system or national health system and so on. There is, however, no reason for these agencies to include in their records data that would be adequate for analysis of the migration process with regard to birthplace etc. and if the information is available it is likely to be of poor quality.

Those interested in migration research can use social surveys to establish, often in much greater detail than the census, the migration characteristics and history of a population. This provides particularly valuable data if a full life history of moves is collected. It is however very expensive and time-consuming and can only realistically be attempted for a small sample of the population. It is likely therefore that such studies will exclude, at least in terms of statistically significant analysis, small populations of immigrants within the larger population.

It is only by survey research that one can begin to approach the question of qualitative data that can determine some of the subjective reasoning that conditioned an individual's decision to move. Although a rich source of data, such enquiries are usually limited by the necessity to review the experience *post hoc* so that it may be difficult to distinguish motive from rationalization of a decision already taken. It is unfortunately rare in migration studies that *before* and *after* data are available which would allow more adequate analysis to be done. However, such enquiries can be supplemented by written evidence during and following the experience of emigration such as letters home and journals and diaries which have proved a valuable historical record of the process of transition and adjustments involved.

Migration and development

It is very clear from what has already been written that the model produced from the analysis of population by census data and by household analysis imposes a number of unreal assumptions about the dynamics of social life. In particular it assumes a stability that is inconsistent with the reality of migratory behaviour. We now can see that neither urban nor rural populations are very stable so far as residence and location of population is concerned. Moreover this apparent stability is often the result of the units within which location is measured: data aggregation may conceal much of the short-distance migration that takes place within given boundaries. It is also important to modify the image that assumes that people only have one residence. The statutory obligations in relation to residence do not prevent people from having second homes or even third or fourth homes; people on regular routine duties may have bi-local residences or may have relatives who can conveniently provide residential alternatives. Particularly this is so in the case of the young and single who may be highly mobile residentially.

Just as there is residential variability so also are there many types and patterns of movement. The same individual may at different stages of his life-cycle be a long-distance and short-distance migrant; he may be a temporary migrant or a seasonal migrant depending on changing circumstances. Equally the assumption that it is the individual who is the unit of analysis has led to false assumptions about the decision processes involved which often are part of a complex process of family decision and strategic selection.

On a world scale we are ready to accept extreme variations of development and modernization between countries but there is a tendency to play down such differences at a national level. Even conceptualizations of stratification which are used to analyse differences in society tend to minimize variation and stress typical characteristics of the class or status aggregates with which they are concerned. Usually such accounts tend to remove the contradictions that arise from social heterogeneity.

Theories of modes of production like other periodization theories have tended to assume that the achievement of modernization or the dominance of a particular mode such as capitalism led almost automatically to the disappearance of everything else. Such theories imply that as soon as the agent of change is introduced an immediate homogenization of the whole society takes place. In reality it is somewhat more profitable to consider the extent to which modes of production coexist despite changes and allow the preservation of pockets of pre-existing relationships to be maintained in spite of the overall domination of a given mode. Thus ancient forms of craft production may be retained among certain sections of the population which have deliberately elected to reject new technology or modes of economic involvement. Gypsies and other migrant people for instance in Europe or the Amish in the United States maintain a livelihood on the fringe of or encapsulated within the dominant form of capitalist society.

The main argument here is to establish the need for explanations of migratory process to take account of the society from which the migrant has come as well as that to which he has gone. This duality of existence raises problems for both immigrants and societies. By which norms is his behaviour to be determined? Even at the formal level where an immigrant is expected to obey the law of the land where he is resident he or she may be unaware of the details of law in such areas as traffic regulations or aspects of family law and may readily contravene a law in the new situation by following a conventional practice in terms of the country of origin.

The dual situation also raises problems for sociologists and others who study migration behaviour. Theoretical models, particularly derived from funtionalist traditions, have tended to assume a model of a unified social whole – a society. By definition the external migrant, at least, is only provided for in the model at one end of the experience. It is difficult, conceptually, for such a theory to hold in tension the two societies to which the migrant, in a real sense, belongs.

In the next section we consider one attempt to overcome this difficulty by a model which attempts to explain the factors causing migration to occur and determining the pattern that it takes.

Classical migration theory

In the middle of the nineteenth century migration theory was dominated by an approach which blended easily into the political economy of the period. Man was rational and as *homo oeconomicus* responded to discernible pressures so as to maximize advantage and minimize discomfort. This Benthamite principle defined a model of migration based on factors of push and pull; those which drove people away from their place of origin and those which acted as attractions to pull them toward somewhere else. The push factors were generally economic and included lack of access to land, lack of employment, low wages, wasted land, drought and famine, population increase. The pull factors offered attractive alternatives to these but in addition contrasted the advantages of the urban to the rural existence, the 'bright lights' and delights available to the urban dweller standing as a beacon to the peasant toiling on the land.

Such a push-pull model addresses only one set of the questions that concern the observer of population movements, those which motivate the individual actor to move. These are important issues, as we shall see, but to focus on them alone is to conceal the extent to which individual actions are embedded in a social fabric that in large measure prepares the individual for the choices available to him, shaping both the opportunities available and the responses that may be made. Thus the exercise of a perfectly free will on which the push-pull model depends is already severely constrained by a sense of the location of the actor in a particular historical and social framework within which his choices are to be made and which gives its particular meanings to the results of these choices. The extent to which people do not appear simply as individual actors is well illustrated in the letter from the Irish mother to her son in the middle of the nineteenth century 'Send home more money, you have another brother'. The mother, in spite of a physical separation of three thousand miles and a separation in time of several weeks, nevertheless sees the emigrant as an extension of the family's strategic possibilities for survival. In spite of our romanticized and 'modern' sense of individual freedom and destiny the son's perception of his continuing involvement and responsibility to the extended family he has left may not be so different and may be shared in any case with his peers in relation to their own families left at home.

The essence of the push-pull model was defined in a paper presented by E. G. Ravenstein to the Royal Statistical Society on 17 March 1885, and a subsequent paper presented in 1889.[3] Both were titled ambitiously *The Laws of Migration* and represent a major attempt at providing some principles to explain the mechanisms of the migration process as he saw it in both an internal and international situation. Ravenstein listed a number of propositions which have remained key elements in a theory that attempted to explain migration by the establishment of flows conditioned by a number of variables. He noted a relationship between migration and distance, distinguishing long and short distance migrants. He

Fig 1. Modified Ravenstein Model

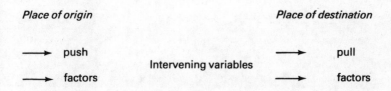

Place of origin   *Place of destination*

⟶ push   ⟶ pull
                        Intervening variables
⟶ factors   ⟶ factors

also showed that although some migration was directly to large
urban centres of attraction there was also a movement by stages
setting in the direction of the centre of attraction. A fourth important factor that Ravenstein noted was the existence of a counter-
stream or counter-flow in any migration situation. Perhaps the
most significant of his findings however lie in his assertions, first
that the development of technology and commerce leads invariably
to an increase in migration, and secondly that of all the motives
producing currents of migration the economic was paramount: 'the
desire inherent in most men to "better" themselves in material
respects'.[4]

The Ravenstein model, in a modified form, has remained the
most significant theoretical contribution based on the assumption
of factors of push and pull. It assumes a set of factors associated
with the area of origin and a set of factors associated with the area of
destination, together with intervening variables which affect the
actual balance of these interests. The model above indicates these
elements. It should be noted that it differs from similar models
such as that of Everett Lee[5] in which the intervening variables are
defined as 'intervening obstacles'. In my view it is more helpful to
treat the intervening variables as both negative and positive
elements in using this model, some frustrating and some enabling
the migrant to reach an intended destination.

This push-pull model is dependent upon a set of assumptions
underlying the balance of interests of the migrant. It assumes a
process of rational decision-making and perfect knowledge of the
system. As we shall see in the next chapter labour market theory

builds on this by concentrating on the economic variables, particularly wage rates, to define migratory activity.

2

LABOUR MARKET THEORY AND MIGRATION

The basic push-pull model for migration behaviour drawn from classical economic theory is closely related to the theory of the labour market. Within this model some of the difficulties of measurement, motivation and interpretation referred to in the last chapter are reduced so as to emphasize supply and demand factors in the provision of labour. In its initial form the model assumed that an equilibrium would be maintained in wage rates because migration would occur to balance differentials caused by the varying advantages of employment locations. Equally in an area from which labour was drawn the model assumed that the diminishing numbers of employees would cause wage rates to rise and thus halt the tendency to migrate.

This model was revised by Keynes in the 1930s when the continued decline of the depressed industrial areas of Britain caused doubts about the capacity of labour mobility to produce an equilibrium, particularly when it was noted that those tending to leave a depressed region were often the most highly skilled. A greater appreciation there also developed of the potential mobility of capital as well as of labour. Consequently the 'disequilibrium theory' called for government intervention to redress the balance by persuading manufacturers to move to declining regions.

As Lind[1] has shown, both these models are deficient. In the first labour is treated as a simple, exchangeable commodity and in the second, although it is recognized as a variable commodity, it is still assumed that the level of wages is the fundamental determinant of the migrant's behaviour. As he suggests, to model migration more realistically one must take account of other economic variables, such as the infrastructure and amenities of the area, distance from other centres of population, the social and cultural image of the area and so on. He also emphasises the point that in a modern economy much migration is motivated by other factors than employment, with the flight from the cities on the one hand and retirement on the other both being important examples of factors outside the labour market.

Once these factors are included the economic model becomes necessarily more complex and more difficult to apply. Without them its use is clearly severely limited by the assumptions on which it rests. In this chapter we consider these assumptions and relate them to three separate migration experiences: the settlement of Australia: migrations within the European region following the Second World War, and internal and interregional migration in Britain.

Before moving to these illustrations let us look in a little more detail at the theory of the labour market in industrial capitalist society. As we indicate above, the development of capitalism brought about a situation in which the worker was 'formerly free' to sell his labour power to the employer within a free market. Consequently within the theories of laissez-faire economics the worker is assumed to be able to exercise choice in the labour market. How much freedom of choice can be exercised and how that choice is perceived remain questions for this model both in regards to the employer as well as for labour. In a useful contribution to labour market analysis in a region of Britain during the mid-1970s, Blackburn and Mann suggest that there are two stages at which workers may be frustrated by the labour market and not experience it as a free market.[2] On the one hand they may simply not possess the knowledge on which to base choice, on the other they may not be able to control the market process in relation to job selection. Buying a job therefore is not the same as buying a dress. You may find that the dress you have chosen and which fits you has in fact been sold to someone else.

These authors note that for the labour market to be truly free it must satisfy a number of conditions. These include a variety of types of employment equally available to all workers; information available to all workers and equally acquired by them; and lastly that there must be a match in the market between preferences and the number of actual jobs. On the demand side the model has assumed that employers stratify the labour market in relation to the productive quality of the labour, the element of human capital that they represent in terms of the skill, training and ability that each worker possesses. It is clear that this model, in whatever form or degree of complexity it appears, is based on a double process of choice by employer and worker.

Such models have been found to be especially inadequate because they assume a holistic and integrated concept of the economy and hence the labour market. An important improvement on the model has been the development of the dual labour market theory which takes account of the major structural differences between the developed, highly profitable and technologically advanced forms of employment and all others. In particular the dual theory provides for an internal labour market from which all but the unskilled manual jobs are filled from inside the existing internal labour market. The advantage of this internal market lies in the fact that it allows for a mutual elimination of risk for worker and employer. The dual labour market implies that for some workers and employers the market is constrained while elsewhere it is free. Certainly the whole question of recruitment from within the known labour force and the differentiation of potential labour on the basis of experience seriously limits any assumption of equality.

Other criticisms of classical economic models, particularly from a Marxist perspective, have developed the idea of a split labour market by elaborating greater degrees of segregation dependent upon an assumption of capitalist divide and rule. From this point of view the interests of capital are best served by keeping an increase in the labour supply, to make use of cheap docile labour with relatively low expectations and aspirations, segmented in such a way that wage rates can be set in relation to non-market factors such as sex, race, ethnicity or age. Similar segmentation and interest in preserving the components are apparent from the perspective of organized labour which has tended to adopt a protectionist attitude toward the internal labour market encouraged by restrictive practices by craft workers and the emphasis on seniority and job protection.

As capitalism has expanded throughout the world it has consistently brought new groups into the labour market. As rural migrants, or overseas immigrants, or women have been absorbed they have started off as an essentially undifferentiated lumpen-proletariat providing undifferentiated labour power for employers who do not place emphasis on levels of skill or capacity, and therefore may not recognize such differentials where they exist. In the early stages of industrialization where promotion or advancement depended upon training, assessment and length of service 'on the job', this was a common situation for the majority of those entering work. As qualifications gained through education and skill training have been developed and their international convertibility enhanced as in the European Common Market, the differentiation and segmentation within the labour market have markedly increased and thus have limited the scope for the unskilled sector of the market.

Another approach which again moves away somewhat from the uniform assumptions of the classical economic theories of the labour market recognizes the differences that exist between different levels and stages of development of industrialization and of capitalism. This approach emphasizes the particular forces at work in each situation that define the characteristics of labour and capital and condition the relations between them. As Roberts[3] shows, industrialization is a different process if it occurs in nineteenth-century Manchester, contemporary Barcelona, or in Lima in Peru. In the first case it is occurring in the centre of an extensive technologically advanced industrial economy, with adequate capital and political power, in the second the economy can be described as semi-peripheral in that it is unevenly developed and foreign capital remains important for development and production, as does imported technology. The third case is one where the internal market is only weakly developed and consequently there is little development of national capital and where agriculture is dominated by peasant production. As Roberts shows in each of these instances the context of industrialization in a particular environment conditions the operation of the labour market and determines the form of the process of industrialization or labour absorption that takes place. In turn therefore it conditions the pattern of migration and the processes used to associate the migrant with the process. This will determine the extent to which migration is temporary or permanent, involves residential settlement and urbanization in association with industrial development, and occurs in a situation of scarcity or over-supply. Similarly, the pattern of state intervention, especially in the area of legislation and controls that affect the operation of the labour market, is likely to vary to the extent to which the state becomes involved directly in the process of industrialization and hence manpower policy.

The process of industrialization and urbanization as it took place in Britain was characterized by the emergence of the factory system. With growing centralization this system absorbed considerable numbers of workers and achieved a stability which allowed and justified expenditure on the infrastructure of extensive working-class housing. Roberts, commenting on Manchester and the area around it in the middle of the nineteenth century, notes a 56.3 per cent increase between 1838 and 1856 in those employed in cotton manufacture, an increase not untypical of expanding labour-intensive industries such as engineering or coal-mining. This expansion was achieved through specific migration patterns:

The labour input into this economy was provided mainly by short-distance migration from the industrialized rural areas; by the early nineteenth century this migration generated an abundant supply of both skilled and unskilled labour. The main source of long-distance migration was Ireland. The Irish were predominantly from a rural background and their initial work was usually unskilled labour, or crafts such as tailoring or shoe-making.[4]

Following writers such as Wallerstein[5] who have argued for the need to look at economic and social phenomena today as part of a world system, Elizabeth Petras[6] has usefully located the movement of labour across national boundaries within this perspective. She argues that the world's division of labour can be described by a division into three interdependent but distinct zones described as core, semi-periphery and periphery. This theory argues that capital, commodities and labour move across national boundaries as part of a developing process that creates complex and inescapable ties of interdependence between countries. Placed in this context, labour migration is explained by the economic and political influence of the core economies over the peripheral and the specific effects of difference in the real and social wage levels in the core and the periphery which leads to recruitment across national boundaries from what is, in effect, an international pool of reserve labour. These moves are regulated by state policies which reflect the same world system of core dominance over the peripheral areas as does the reaction of the system to cyclical rhythms and secular trends in the world economy as a whole.

The most specific relationship established from this perspective and supported by work outside it such as that of Brinley Thomas[7] is the relationship between the flow of labour and the flow of capital. This relationship has served to confirm the inequalities already present in the world system by emphasizing the advantages of dominance in relation to both labour and capital access.

From this perspective the periphery is historically characterized as the supplier of raw materials and primary products to the industries of the core economies. The supplying countries remain limited to mono-production and lack the capital to develop an industrial infrastructure, having to buy back consumer goods from the core, thus emphasizing and confirming their dependency. In consequence the relatively low-waged and unskilled labour in the peripheral countries remains as a huge reserve for the core countries who experience seasonal or critical labour shortage. This pool however is not equally accessible or equally accessed. Not only political controls but often quite specific political agreements may be entered into between sending and receiving countries to channel and regulate this labour flow. A striking example is the agreement between Turkey and West Germany to encourage the emigration of Turkish workers to West Germany in the period since the early 1960s. It is worth noting that this movement was seen by the Turkish government as an essential part of their plan to stabilize population growth and encourage economic growth. Similar arrangements using the established administrative system occurred with most of the former imperial European states in relation to their former colonies and dependencies in the third world following the Second World War.

Apart from formal or semi-formal schemes, other factors condition the potential flow of migrants from the semi-periphery to the core. Perhaps the most salient of these factors is geographic proximity. Where there is an adjacent peripheral or semi-peripheral economy next to or contiguous with an advanced core economy this cuts down on many of the problems of communication, ease of return home, transport and associated costs of transfer. It is notable that in many of the major contemporary movements this is true. As Petras states (p. 56): 'The greatest number of foreign workers in Sweden are from Finland; in Switzerland from Italy; in the US from Mexico and Canada; in Argentina from Chile and Paraguay; in Venezuela from Colombia; and in South Africa from Mozambique and Lesotho.' One might add nearer home, in the United Kingdom from Ireland, where despite heavy migration in the period following the Second World War the Irish-born remain the largest minority population in Britain. Apart from proximity, cultural affinity, especially language affinity, may be important in conditioning migration flows, as may the extent of racial or ethnic prejudice against certain groups. Common legal and religious codes are also important in mediating the flow, as are conventions with regard to entry arrangements for the families of the primary labourers who are being imported. A further factor of some importance is the question of remittances which may play a significant role in some of the economies of the sending countries on the periphery. In 1976, for instance, remittances from nationals working in the Middle East formed the single largest source of foreign exchange in Pakistan, and in the West Indies in the early 1960s and also in Ireland they formed between 2 and 5 per cent of the gross domestic product.

It should also be noted that migration is selective within the peripheral countries and will tend to draw most heavily from the periphery of the periphery, that is those areas most heavily disadvantaged in the sending countries, unless selective criteria are applied.

These movements between core and periphery may form part of a wider penetration by the core of the periphery. In his excellent account of the development of the United Kingdom, Hechter[8] shows the strategies used by the English government to exert economic, political and cultural dominance over the peripheral countries of Scotland, Wales and Ireland. This process involved not only the recruitment of peripheral labour but the establishment of colonists within the periphery. This process, which forms the context within which migration takes place, can be achieved by coercion of slave or indentured labour, colonial settlement or transportation through which significant groups of the core population are settled in the periphery or by highly selective recruitment of talented manpower from the periphery to the centre.

These considerations of labour market theory essentially distinguish two approaches to the problems of the migration of labour. In the first example that we considered, defined by models derived from laissez-faire economics, the social actor is the individual worker taking a free choice in relation to the opportunities available in the labour market. It remains part of the assumption of these models that the individual has a property in his own person; a characteristic derived from Hobbes which as McPherson shows,[9] dominates the political theory of capitalist political economy. Ultimately, from this perspective, migration is caused by individual (formally free) decision makers responding to market opportunities. There is also an assumption, following Hegel, that the interests of the state and the individual are in the last instance essentially similar and the framework for analysis tends to be defined by the boundaries of the state in which the individual has his origins.

The second theoretical perspective that we have considered developed by Wallerstein and his followers assumes the existence of a highly complex interdependent world economic system within which the exchange of labour forms a part. This system is stratified in terms of the relative power, wealth and technological advantage of the core economies over the periphery. Consequently the characteristics of the labour market as it appears to potential emigrants is conditioned by this stratification of opportunity and advantage. While not wholly determinate of the decision-making process, this view suggests that decisions are not taken in a free and neutral market but rather that the constraints and opportunities in the market at any given time have to be understood as specific market conditions that arise from the broader relations and contradictions of world capitalism.

Each of these views leads to a distinctive emphasis with regard to the formulation of migration flows. The first view tends toward an emphasis on the determinants of decision and motivation on the part of the migrant and consequently corresponds more closely to an action perspective in sociological terms. The second corresponds to a structuralist perspective in that it places emphasis on the external factors within the labour market itself that shape the market, limit perfect knowledge on the part of the actors, or create bias in the decision-making process. As we shall show in the next chapter, both of these views are necessary and corrective to each other.

Migration to Australia over the long sea routes

The earliest settlers who landed in Botany Bay on 18 January 1788 and established the first settlement at Sydney Cove consisted of a governor and his staff, some 200 marines with, in some instances, wives and children and nearly 800 convicts of whom about 200 were women. The settlement, which arose from the landing in Botany Bay during Captain Cook's voyage in 1770, was intended as a penal colony specifically to provide a suitable location for transportation of criminals, in part replacing the American Colonies which had been used for this purpose until 1775. Although more convicts arrived, it was not until 1797 that a policy was introduced of allowing those who had completed the term of their sentences to be emancipated but where appropriate be given a land grant. The colony developed slowly and amidst great hardship because of inadequate supplies and support from the homeland. The earliest free enterprise development came with the grant to some of the military in control of the colony and the development of a ring of officers who developed an active speculation in land and the cargoes of ships coming to the colony. Meanwhile the population continued to increase with additional shipments of prisoners now mainly convicted of political offences. Many of these convicts were Scots and Irish supporters of the French Revolution and the 1798 Rebellion in Ireland.

This brief account describes an initial colonization by forced labour which gradually gave way in the 1790s to the possibility that free settlers could also take advantage of the opportunity offered by the new colony. Inducements were offered by the British government of free land and for the first two years of free convict labour, though initially few took advantage of this opportunity. Similar assisted passages were arranged for numbers of single women together with the large-scale assisted passages for urban working-class men and women during the 1830s and 1840s. By 1850 the population of New South Wales which was still the only effectively colonized area amounted to over a quarter of a million, most of whom were settled in the urban area of Sydney. Following the discovery of gold in the area near Melbourne a rush of emigrants from Britain flocked to Australia – no longer as assisted emigrants but somehow finding their passage money and getting themselves to the gold fields.

This pattern of free migration continued predominantly from Britain until the end of the century. Although the gold rush was relatively short-lived, growing opportunities in Australia and New Zealand gave opportunity to European migrants. Until 1891 they consisted of one settler from the rest of Europe to every nine from Britain, in the next fifty years until 1940 the ratio had become one to five Britons and since 1947 at the end of the Second World War two out of every three immigrants were from the rest of Europe, predominantly the southern European countries bordering the Mediterranean. The concentration of immigrants from these countries, building on patterns established at the beginning of the twentieth century, created remarkably localized Italian, Greek, Albanian and Slav communities that reflected to a high degree the community life and associations and cultural traditions that they had left at home. By effective chain-migration they sent money home to pay the fares of relatives in the home village or district to follow the forerunners out. Price[10] who has made a particular study of this group, notes that, unlike the British settlers who were drawn largely from the urban working class, the Southern Europeans were predominantly peasants and fishermen from the villages and small towns. He shows how through the process of chain-migration a remarkable homogeneity was maintained in the new situation and this significantly had effects in the stratification of Australian society. Southern Europe provided the majority of rural settlers, small shopkeepers and entrepreneurs. They were received with considerable hostility by the British Australians in spite of the fact that there was little direct economic competition. But here we are already starting to discuss aspects of the process of settlement and assimilation and can safely leave this dimension to later chapters.

This very brief account of the settlement of Australia over a period of less than two hundred years illustrates a number of issues with regard to labour market theory and migration. With a relatively small and widely scattered indigenous population Australia was effectively a fresh start for European settlers. Thus the use of convict labour supported by troops allows for the deliberate policy of the British state to use transportation as an opportunity to solve problems of social order by forced emigration. In an inverse manner this can be seen as an extension of the need for social control in the reorientation of the labour market in Britain. From this point of view it does not accord well with the model of free decision in a neutral market. Although the situation developed towards one of free migration and settlement this was conditioned by the considerable distance and consequent cost of passage until the present century.

As the history of colonization unfolds and settlements become established, Australia develops autonomy as a state independent within the British Commonwealth. At this point the interests of the Australian state and its requirements in establishing a population policy consistent with the needs of its own labour market become paramount and selection becomes increasingly related to Australian requirements rather than reciprocating the needs or opportunities of the European homelands. Increasingly selective of the labour it requires, Australia can be seen to be participating in a world market which conditions its migration policy.[11]

Recent migration within Europe

The post-war period of reconstruction in Europe saw the promotion of extensive immigration into the core European countries. Britain recruited Irish workers so that by the beginning of the 1960s there were almost a million Irish-born in England and Wales. In 1973 France and West Germany each had some two and a half million foreign workers representing some 10 per cent of the labour force. Thirty per cent of the labour force in Switzerland and Luxembourg, 7 per cent of that of Belgium and Sweden and about 2 per cent of the Dutch labour force were foreign born. These numbers conceal to a certain extent the actual numbers of immigrants into the core European countries. Algerians returned to France as French nationals as did Maltese to Britain and Indonesians to Holland and a certain number of nationals from the Congo to Belgium. There were in addition a significant number of 'illegal' immigrants.

After 1973 the effects of the oil crisis limited the flows of immigrant workers, particularly from countries outside the EEC, and where few new jobs were being filled by immigrants some of those originally considered as temporary migrants were being permitted to stay and bring in their families. Thus the original rationale of foreign worker importation was compromised so far as the importing countries were concerned, since the main advantage of a temporary importation of foreign workers under contract lay in the capacity to use this measure to adjust to uncertainties in the economic cycle caused by fluctuations in the market and the reluctance of the indigenous labour force to take employment in the low-paid, low-status and less-attractive jobs. Gradually the immigrants had infiltrated most sections of the economy and as Salt[12] points out the effect of migration of the 'Gästarbeiter' or guest workers, was to make more rigid the occupational distinctions between the indigenous labour force and the immigrants, with the result that when the recession came the redundancies among foreign workers were not as great as had been expected. In any case many of the unemployed foreign workers stayed on in the host country and although initially after 1973 their unemployment rate was higher than that of the indigenous workforce this situation did not persist in either France or Germany.

The significance of these migrations in post-war Europe generally can be shown by looking at more detailed effects. West Germany for instance in the two years 1959–60 had a net immigration of over 500 thousand. In France there was a net immigration of 1430 thousand in the four years 1960–63. Similarly in the United Kingdom in the earlier period 1958–63 (mid-year) there was a net immigration of 443 thousand. Although the French situation is partly explained by repatriation from North Africa the numbers are considerable and it is notable that in the fifteen years between 1965 and 1980 immigration accounted for half of the population expansion in Germany and one fifth of that for Britain.[13]

As figure 2 indicates this post-war immigration has been charac-

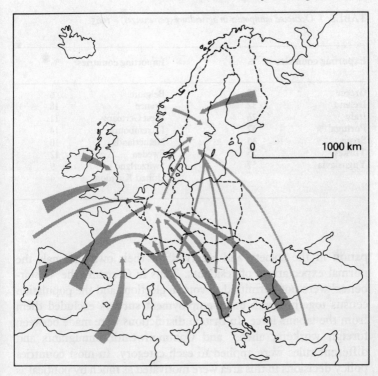

Fig. 2 Post-war migration flows in Europe showing flows from the periphery and old colonies to the centre

terized by a movement from the European periphery to the core countries in the centre. The countries of immigration are confined to north-western Europe and to the most heavily industrialized and urbanized areas within them. Conversely the sending countries have been, for the most part, those with a high proportion of the labour force still engaged in agriculture. Table 1 distinguishes the exporting and the importing countries as they stood in 1965 and indicates clearly the differences in economic structure between core and periphery.

The European labour-importing countries adopted very varied and distinctive strategies with regard to immigrant labour. Some like Switzerland and initially West Germany imposed rigid restrictions on the length of stay of migrants and limited their partici-

TABLE 1 *Occupied manpower in agriculture (percentages) – 1965*

Exporting countries	%	Importing countries	%
Greece	55	Belgium	6
Ireland	32	France	18
Italy	26	West Germany	11
Portugal	42	Luxembourg	14
Spain	35	Netherlands	10
Turkey	75	Sweden	12
Yugoslavia	57	Switzerland	9
		United Kingdom	4

pation in the society and reserved for their own nationals the normal expectations of residents. Thus in Germany the 'Gästarbeiter' were not permitted to vote in elections and the population census together with other employment surveys excluded them from the labour force. In Britain distinctions were made between foreign workers, aliens, and Commonwealth immigrants and different rules were applied to each category. In most countries policy decisions in this area were motivated as much by political as by economic decisions and altered over the period of the heaviest inflows as the result of changing circumstances in the labour market and in the national climate. A good example of this change is recorded by Rose[14] in relation to Switzerland, which brought in a specific policy to reduce the number of foreign workers in 1964 and again in 1967. Rose[15] writes:

Political reasons were more important than economic ones in creating this policy . . . The percentage of foreign workers in the labor force had risen to 32 per cent and the percentage was accelerating: the Swiss feared Überfremdung (over-foreignization). By 1960 the majority of foreigners (79 per cent) were Catholics and mostly Italian (59 percent); the Swiss feared an imbalance in their traditional religious and linguistic composition.

The implications of migration policy will be discussed more fully in Chapter 5. It should be noted here that even where labour market considerations may operate at the initial stages of policy implementation other factors also intervene in relation to the reception of immigrant labour, and labour market considerations must be mediated in regard to the sending countries. In all of the countries that we are considering, major economic restructuring was taking place. As well as movement between countries there was a considerable regional redistribution within the importing countries, though clearly none of them had any longer a sufficient rural base from which the needs of development and industrialization could be met solely within their own boundaries.

Although the migration of workers from Turkey or Sicily or Ireland can be accommodated within the terms of the push-pull model, particularly when the move could be considered as temporary and was eased by direct job recruitment in the sending country, this model does not readily adapt to the varied policies which different countries developed to accommodate the recruitment and adaptation process. In almost every case the state as the agency regulating entry devised controls and licensing mechanisms that conditioned the operations of employers, limited the occupational areas in which the immigrant workers could be initially employed and imposed limitations of stay or work permits to ensure the temporary nature of the visit. Increasingly the European states found that they were under pressure to adopt more restrictive practices for the protection of their own nationals while at the same time wishing to preserve maximum flexibility in the labour market. This contradictory situation was somewhat enhanced by the development among the Scandinavian countries and in the European Community of common labour markets based on the idea of a free movement of labour with a consequent limitation on the capacity for individual states to modify the market conditions. The consequent contradiction in objectives has been exaggerated in the case of the European Community by expansion to include labour-exporting countries like Ireland and Greece. This process is taken a step further by the inclusion of Spain and Portugal as members.

In a thoughtful and perceptive report for the OECD by Hunter and Reid[16] it is shown that the operations of the free labour market are rarely sufficient to accommodate the needs of the market to recruit or the needs of labour to volunteer itself on to the market.

As they point out:

> Mobility is not a homogeneous entity but a concept which incorporates a variety of responses to situations of imbalance. Because of this diversity, it is misleading to think in terms of mobility as a whole; rather we must work on the basis of particular problems, such as geographical or occupational mobility . . . While voluntary mobility is in most cases desirable and should form a basis for mobility policy by itself it may be inadequate or too prolific in relation to the economy's needs for labour redistribution.[17]

These remarks, while addressed primarily to the redistribution of labour between regions and occupational sectors, have also salience for the post-war recruitment of foreign workers within Europe. The difficulties of viewing this complex movement either as simply a phenomenon of the labour market or as the policy outcome of simple contractual interchange between sovereign states in the core and on the periphery is evident. Even where such arrangements existed they did not operate without the interplay between the immigrant and the wider market forces that lay behind the policy developments. Inevitably these actors must take decisions within the framework of a set of assumptions that represent both a policy of one or more governments and an apparently free market. While the free market is clearly neither free nor equal, nor is the policy formulated fully or capable of the degree of regulation of movement that would be necessary if the policy was to be wholly effective. Rather it is a matter of *ad hoc* responses which can, after the event, be seen to be rather more coherent than they ever are while they emerge. Commenting on the development of reciprocal arrangements with regard to social security provisions that had developed between the Irish Republic and the United Kingdom the present author found:

> . . . administrative needs such as those affecting taxation, social security, unemployment and pension benefits tend to bring together governments whose citizens are participating in either permanent or temporary migration. If, as in the Irish case, there are no controls on entry or exit these administrative arrangements tend to become more complex and inclusive of the immigrant and to differentiate him less in legal and administrative terms from the native-born.[18]

For the most part, at least initially, the migrant is little protected or supported. He is available to be exploited and is in general willing to exploit the relatively better situation that he finds himself in. As John Berger and Jean Mohr show in their evocative account *Seventh Man*, the migrant is defined as a member of an underclass by both managers and trade unions:

For capitalism migrant workers fill a labor shortage in a specially convenient way. They accept the wages offered and in doing so, slow down wage increases in general . . . The migrant is in several other ways an 'ideal' worker. He is eager to work overtime. He is willing to do shiftwork at night. He arrives politically innocent – that is to say without any proletarian experience . . . Any individual migrant who does become a leader or 'militant' can be immediately and easily expelled from the country. The trade unions are unlikely to defend him. Migrants pay taxes and social security contributions but will not draw many benefits during their temporary residence. Their cost to the system in terms of social capital can be kept to a minimum.[19]

The advantages of temporary migration to both migrant and employer depend upon the assumption that it is temporary. For the migrant the relatively high earnings can permit not only remittances to support the family at home but also savings to allow a nest-egg of capital to be brought back with him when he returns. If the time away is short he is prepared to suffer the deprivation of family and friends and the long hours and discomforts involved in his employment.

Once the migrant changes his perspective, becomes adapted to the new society and no longer sees a place for himself in the home community it becomes much more difficult to support the illusion and the temporary expedient becomes for both migrant and host country a permanent commitment.

Internal migration in Britain

Some of the factors involved in developing a policy for regional adjustment in relation to the development of the labour market can be seen in the United Kingdom since the development of the recession and the very high rates of unemployment that have characterized the economy since the end of the 1970s. There has been a conscious attempt to influence the market in favour of less developed regions or areas of decline of traditional industry, but these factors do not operate in isolation. As Lind points out, considerable internal movement within Britain and between regions is due not to labour market factors as such but from a desire to move away from areas of congestion in the cities or to move away from the cities altogether. Similarly the changing patterns of public and private transport; the provisions of elements of infrastructure such as motorways and extensions to rail systems, have altered the commuting patterns around major cities and in particular London. Lind suggests that in this case new industry may be following change in residence particularly in the South East of England which, at the time of his comment (1969) was an area of high growth of employment. He warns, however, against accepting a simple one-to-one causal relationship. 'It is much more likely that the relationships are complex, and that the causal nexus is at least partly cumulative. In part at least, the same factors which have caused people to move out of London – congestion, high land prices, etc – influence industry for many of the same reasons.'[20]

The work of Blackburn and Mann considering the local labour market that they studied in the Cambridge region confirms this degree of complexity. These authors show that the operation of the market so far as the exercise of choice by workers is concerned is a good deal more complex than simply the calculation of wage differentials. What they reveal is a climate of opinion that exists in a community with regard to the possibility of employment in each specific firm. This climate is made up of accumulated information and opinion which incorporates a wide range of factors in addition to wage rates and overtime opportunities.

However, it is factors outside the specific relationship to employment that have to be considered in conjunction with them. Most of the European cities, partly as the result of war damage and partly because of the age and inadequacy of existing housing stock, had to embark on rehousing programmes that included deliberate attempts at creating new towns outside the major conurbations and clearing existing slum housing. These effects were also relevant to the decision to move and indeed the priority of housing as a problem faced by newcomers in the large cities shows that it is an important associated factor in internal relocation. An example is given by Alberoni[21] in a description of the situation in Italy where he points out the symbiotic relationship that develops between the rural sending area and the city.

The internal migration in Italy, then, does not consist of an unobtrusive series of isolated departures of people who have arrived at their individual decisions under increasing pressure from individual difficulties; it arises out of the spreading of new ambitions and a new vision of one's present state in relation to what one could be in another society developing along different lines; it is the upsurge, gradual at first but growing stronger, of a new social perspective, a new prospect of livelihood which eventually leads to the individual feeling estranged from his own community while he belongs in spirit to another which, although still in the process of development, already has a structure and a definite identity. It is above all young people who are involved, but older age groups are not excluded; not only men but women are concerned; the process is set in motion at first by concrete possibilities and information about what is happening near at hand . . . The urge to leave stems not so much from a rejection of ones own place in the community as a rejection of the community and its structure. Those who depart do not go in search of work which will allow them to save one day, nor are they seeking their fortunes in order to return later and take up a more advantageous position in the community. Those who leave go in search of a different way of life, another society in which they can fulfill themselves more completely, with reference to new values with which they must, therefore, have been in sympathy before their departure.

Internal migration may be influenced by decisions nationally or locally regarding housing or location of industrial or tertiary sector development. Manpower policies have increasingly endeavoured to integrate these elements in relation to general and sectoral needs. Like other European countries the information base that would permit a comprehensive analysis of either job changes or residential change is not really adequate. The OECD report on manpower in the United Kingdom in 1968 admitted that it was not possible to distinguish how many of the 8 million moves have been in the interest of higher productivity and which of them had the opposite effect.[22]

The lack of adequate statistics to assess the detail of movement has long been a problem in relation to some coordination of such policies in relation to regional development and location. New regional boundaries were defined in 1974 and since then comprehensive figures have been calculated on the basis of the new regions and published in the Demographic Review issued by the Office of Population Censuses and Surveys in Great Britain. Table 2 shows the rates of population change in those new standard regions in three periods attributable to migration as distinct from natural increase (excess of births over deaths).

TABLE 2 *Rates of population change in standard regions (per thousand per year) not attributable to natural increase*

	1961–66	1966–71	1971–76
Northern	−5.6	−3.6	−1.8
Yorkshire and Humberside	−0.4	−2.8	−0.4
East Midlands	2.7	1.6	2.9
East Anglia	5.7	8.8	11.1
South East	1.2	−2.1	−2.9
Greater London	−11.0	−14.7	−12.6
South West	6.7	5.4	8.2
West Midlands	−0.9	−0.7	−1.7
North West	−1.7	−2.5	−2.5
England	0.6	−0.8	−0.4
Wales	0.1	−0.8	2.7
Scotland	−6.9	−5.2	−2.2
Great Britain	−0.2	−1.3	−0.4

Note: These figures include changes in armed forces and balancing adjustments but effectively show internal and external effects of migration on each region. Office of Population Censuses and Surveys, 1978, *Demographic Review 1977, Great Britain*, London, HMSO, p. 4 Table 1.3. See also for Chapters 5, 6 and 7 on international migration, population distribution and implications of demographic trends.

Internal mobility may arise from a variety of changes in social circumstance. In many cases it may be the result of a change of employment but very often such moves are related to particular labour markets and are selective in relation to them rather than simply an open move in search of work. In other cases the search for work may be secondary to a move achieved for reasons of housing or health or to be near kin or for retirement. The extent of internal mobility must be related to programmes of housebuilding and slum clearance, planning decisions and policies for provision of the social infrastructure. Migration will in any case vary according to the stage of the life-cycle of the potential migrant and the changing pattern of family development and dispersal.

The introduction of a question in the 1966 Census asking for place of residence one year before has greatly improved our capacity to establish patterns of internal movement. That census showed over 5 million residential moves during the year before the enumeration and in the same period the Ministry of Labour estimated that 8 million people in Britain changed their employer. If we assume this figure it represents a turnover of about 40 per cent per annum of the total occupied population.

Internal mobility analysis in Britain is greatly complicated by the problems posed by boundary changes and the definition of what constitutes a significant move in terms of distance, duration and change in other social variables. In much the same way as the executive may stay in any Hilton Hotel throughout the world and expect to find the same basic furniture in the room, so with the expansion of communication routes and inter-city linkages the relationship between work, residence and social provision may for some groups in the population have had less significance than they have in the past.

Writing in 1969, Lind was able to argue that the overall regional strategy in Britain was still governed by the Keynesian model of regional disequilibrium. 'Just as the unthinking acceptance of the laissez faire model in the twenties and thirties hampered effective relief operations in those parts of Britain dependent on declining industries, so it is arguable that the present tendency to halt emigration at almost any cost delays the creation of an integrated strategy for regional welfare'.[23] In 1984 the high levels of unemployment and the severe regional effects on those declining industries suggest that the problems of regional disequilibrium remain a central issue for social policy and social research.

3

MIGRATION DECISIONS AND SOCIAL CHANGE

In this chapter we consider the determinants of migration from a perspective which, while recognizing the force of labour market theory, assumes a more expanded model of determination and social action to explain the process of migration. In developing this approach it is assumed that individual acts are social events located in particular historically specific circumstances. These circumstances condition decisions but do not determine them without the active participation of individuals.[1]

Migration decisions

The decision to move has been described as a little like the decision to marry. All of the pre-disposing circumstances may be available but it still takes a particular recognition of circumstances and a confirming proposal and acceptance to bring the matter to a head. As Bourdieu indicates, although our social acts may correspond to social rules they still involve a strategy of choice and timing in obeying them.[2] There is an element of uncertainty built into the choice. Will she say yes? What if she says no? Should I go? Or should I stay?

Too often the push-pull model has been used only in a context that takes account of individual decision on the basis of rational choice. But the rational choice of the migrant is only the immediate apparent cause; the underlying causes which predetermine the choice situation are specific events which have brought the migrant to the point of decision – often without him being aware of them. These events are not immediately available to cost benefit analysis of the advantages of going or staying.

Migration is clearly a selective process. In situations of voluntary migration not everyone goes, although the differences between goers and stayers may not be very evident to us. The factors of push and pull appear the same for a particular age group sharing a common position in the place of origin. What appears to determine the difference may be whether or not there is, in a particular family, a tradition of moving or staying. Thus there is evidence to suggest that migration may be selective between families as well as between individuals. Though families may be found quite commonly in Ireland in which all of the children, or all but one of the children, have emigrated, there will be others in apparently equal circumstances in which the children have all remained in the locality. Especially where there is a long-sustained process of migration, cause and effect become difficult to separate. Migration can and does become a normal and expected process where the example of those who have already migrated is available and where family and social life has become conditioned to continual reorganization as members move away.

There are in any case specific methodological difficulties involved in exploring motivation. If we ask a potential population if they intend to migrate we cannot be sure if those who say yes will actually do so. If we ask those who have migrated why they did so they may rationalize a decision already taken. In either case if we are to rely on the migrant's responses we must assume that his motives are apparent to him, and the 'stated' motives are the 'real' ones.

In general these difficulties lead to some imputation of motives based on the evidence of structural factors using an elaborated set of push and pull variables. Additional strength may be added if we can distinguish factors which particularly affect different types of migrant in a given population. Thus Touraine and Ragazzi[3] distinguish *départ* involving conscious and deliberate choice from *déplacement* when an opportunity gives rise to an intention, which may or may not have been latent, and lastly *mobilité* which is the result of aspirations of vertical mobility. In another study of 200 Dutch emigrants Wenholt devises a model of nine categories of migration based on motivational structure. Similarly Taylor in studying the moves of Durham miners distinguishes four types of motivational structure which he describes as Resultant – usually the move is the result of redundancy; Aspiring – strong sense of seeking an alternative life; Dislocated – already detached from the community; and Epiphenomenal – a diverse variety of factors.[4] Such typologies have the advantage that they can assist analysis without foreclosing the options that can be addressed in the empirical situation. As Wenholt claims: 'At least it guarantees a measure of respect for the diversity and complexity of the real facts'.[5]

Such approaches can be helpful in establishing a grasp on the variety of forms that migration takes and its characteristics. But we are not only concerned with varieties of motivation but also varieties of circumstance and structures which alter over time and are themselves affected by the act of migration that is in part stimulated by them.

Social change

In order to appreciate the dynamics of migration it is important to locate it as a process within a broader consideration of social change. Clearly migration is itself an act of change for the migrant as well as each of the societies between which he moves. This process is cumulative in relation to the extent of the migration and the numbers who participate in it. It will also vary in relation to the pattern of selection and the effect that differential selection may have on the population at either end of the transition process. In demographic terms the age and sex structure may be substantially altered and this may distort the age and sex balance if there is a specific and sustained flow. Apart from demographic consider- ations the implications for the social, cultural and economic life of the community at each end of the spectrum must be considered. However, it is not enough to consider the process simply horizont- ally; it has a vertical dimension as well which is apparent in the structure of family and community life. Not only are there dimen- sions that affect the immediate migrants but also there are implications for their successors in both communities. The act of migration therefore redefines a history and must be considered in its historical dimension, affecting a broad climate of relationships in time as well as space.

A useful attempt at a model which permits us to hold these dimensions together has been developed from the original paper of Zelinsky[6] by Daniel Courgeau in relation to France.[7] In considering spatial mobility over a period of three centuries he is able to relate migration not only to different historical periods within which it takes different forms but also to its varying effects on different institutions within the society. In covering three hundred years of history he is able to show the way in which spatial mobility alters in relation to the development of new social forms. In the first stage the society is essentially traditional; the relation between births and deaths is fairly well balanced and consequently migration is rare, apart from fulfilling the needs of marriage. Only a select group in the population are likely to travel further afield. These are mainly merchants, seamen, soldiers, the aristocracy and students. Except in times of war the majority of the population never moves beyond the boundaries of the immediate known world of their community and district.

In the second place in this demographic transition there is a fairly rapid decline in the death rate while the birth rate remains high. In consequence there is a rapid increase in population and a fresh consideration of space which is characterized by alterations in land tenure and a more productive mode of agricultural production. Since land becomes a premium the opportunity afforded by the discovery of land overseas or the acquisition of land by conquest provides an additional safety valve. Such settlements as the Australian one we have already considered or the early settlements of North and South America by Europeans were achieved through military strength and coincidental introduction of diseases against which the indigenous populations had no resistance.

Courgeau sees associated with this second stage the growth of industrial towns near to coal or ore deposits or on trade routes, but he emphasizes that it is the international opportunities for agricultural settlement that are the first response to population growth. The move to the cities really belongs to the third phase when the birthrate drops and population growth stabilizes. It is during this phase that the introduction of new techniques in agriculture makes possible the release of population to the cities and this stage is usually marked by a decline in international emigration. With the fourth phase there develops a situation of little or no population growth since both the birth rate and the death rate have been stabilized at a low level as the result of control over fertility. Such international migration as occurs is highly selective of skilled manpower needed in the developing countries. Reverse flows of migration are stimulated from these countries which still have surplus population. The drift from country to town becomes less, there are more moves between cities and new forms of temporary mobility such as commuting or travelling as part of employment assume greater significance. This model, while clearly imprecise in relation to specific historical conditions, is used to support Courgeau's view that we should not anticipate an even or consistent transition. As he points out:

This theory also has the merit of showing not only that different countries are at different stages of their transition but also that the various regions within a particular country are not necessarily at the same point either. Looked at in spatial terms, this model of mobility extends from capital cities to the most remote areas and is transmitted by the flow of previously settled migrants and the flow of ideas and innovations.[8]

Clearly such a model must be related to the specific circumstances of each country and each region but it provides a valuable start in relating migration to social change. It is used by Courgeau in relation to three blocks of time; the eighteenth century, the period from the French Revolution to the Second World War and the period since the Second World War. While clearly built around a broad notion of demographic transition, the value of the analysis lies in the relationship between migration and the associated concepts of space and time related to it and the changing character of the major institutions. This can be well illustrated in relation to the marriage and family patterns which during the eighteenth century were characterized by very localized intermarriage with 60 per cent of rural marriages and 85 per cent of urban marriages being between partners from the same commune. This situation had not altered significantly by 1830 but after that date there was a major change. Considering the pattern of endogamy for the Ardéche he finds a move from 60 per cent in 1830 to 52 per cent in 1865 to 35 per cent in 1935 and only 30 per cent at the end of the Second World War. Although the drop was not as great for the cities, he nevertheless concludes that by the end of the Second World War more than half of the marriages involved migration.

Such a change in family construction implies changes also in economic and political relationships, in leisure, religion and education and consequently in the use of space. Growing incorporation of state activities like the police and the army, especially the introduction of general conscription, had important effects in mixing the population and developing a sense of nationalism to replace the localism that had characterized the earlier period. Ultimately after the First World War controls were placed on foreign immigration, first by employers' organizations and ultimately, after the Second World War, by the state itself. A good indication of these changes can be given by comparing two of the maps used in Courgeau's study which contrast the proportion of non-native population in each department in 1861 (Fig. 3a) and 1946 (Fig. 3b).[9]

The period since the Second World War in Courgeau's study shows a rapid run down of the primary sector of agricultural and fishing employment from 37.9 per cent in 1946 to 9.5 per cent in 1975; in the same period there was a rapid increase in the tertiary sector which rose from 32.3 per cent in 1946 to 51.3 per cent in 1975. The consequences of these changes were dramatic in the increase in seasonal migrants for agricultural work from 10,000 in 1946 to 130,000 in 1975.

Now the French experience that we have outlined here over three centuries depicts a scenario of major social change in which migration at all times is a central component. Change in the physical location of individuals brings about changes in those locations. A migrant son or daughter increases a family's universe of action. Migration is an essential ingredient of the process of industrialization, of the shifts in agricultural production and of national incorporation. The development of the nuclear family is the development of a type of family that permits great spatial mobility, that is not tied to land or kin and constrained by obligations to a specific locality and social milieu.

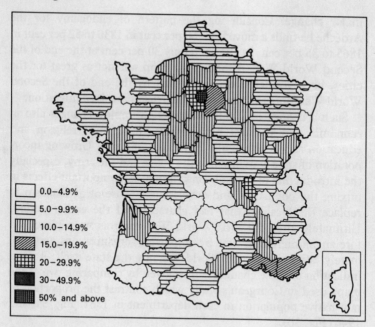

Fig. 3(a) Proportion of non-native population in each department in 1861

The map legend reads:

0.0–4.9%
5.0–9.9%
10.0–14.9%
15.0–19.9%
20–29.9%
30–49.9%
50% and above

In Britain the same kind of development can be observed also and here Hechter's study *Internal Colonialism* covering the period from 1536 until 1966 is a useful guide.[10] Although Hechter is less interested in migration as such he shows how with the development of the British state the relationship to the peripheral Celtic fringe led to the development of specific policies of incorporation that involved population mobility spatially in both directions and also qualitatively and conceptually as the cultural, economic and political dominance of the centre was achieved. Hechter also notes that one of the characteristic features of the development of industrial society is the separation of the individual from the social roots and cultural cocoon that formerly gave him definition. He quotes Gellner's very useful discussion of nationalism where he writes:

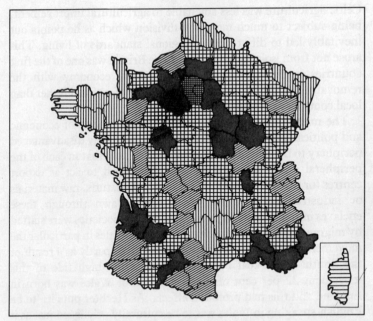

(b) Proportion of non-native population in each department in 1946

If a man is not firmly set in a social niche, he is obliged to carry his identity with him, in his whole style of conduct and expression; in other words his 'culture' becomes his identity. And the classification of men by 'culture' is of course the classification by 'nationality'. It is for this reason that it now seems inherent in the very nature of things that to be human means to have some nationality. In our particular social context, it *is* inherent in the nature of things.[11]

Hechter describes the process of national development in Britain in terms of an uneven wave of industrialization over territorial space that in turn leads to the consolidation of the unequal distribution of resources between core and periphery. He argues that the super-ordinate core group achieves its dominance by enforcing both social and cultural division of labour. Prior to the industrial revolution the distinction between the different regions in the British Isles was due largely to highland and lowlands, with the Celts as the conquered race disproportionately clustered in the highland zone.

Celtic agriculture was less amenable to agricultural improvement, being subject to much more sub-division which as he points out inevitably led to differences in regional standards of living. This arose not from isolation, however, since Britain was one of the first countries in Europe to achieve a national economy with the removal of local tariffs and the maintenance of national rather than local control over weights and measures.

The main migrations associated with this process of economic and political incorporation were from the relatively disadvantaged periphery to the core, but it is important to note that in each of the peripheral areas industrial enclaves developed to act as export centres for the narrow range of exports of foodstuffs, raw materials or industrial commodities which were drawn through these enclaves into the centre. The regional enclave societies were staffed by migrants in the opposite direction and in Wales in particular the movement into the periphery was substantial, partly as a result of the South Wales coal boom. In 1911 at the high tide of this movement 22 per cent of the population of Wales was born in England and this had profound effects. As Hechter puts it: 'to be English-speaking in Wales was to be culturally privileged just as it is today in neo-colonial cities like Accra or Lagos. It was a mark of status and an entrance to privileged company. Englishmen in Wales were in this sense akin to a colonial elite.'[12] Hechter's analysis shows that migrations such as these have to be related to processes of internal and external change in relationships at the economic, political, religious, social, and cultural levels. In each of these domains the act of migration can be interpreted as part of a process of development which is often uneven in its effects and leads to the power and capacity of the centre to exploit the peripheral regions and increases its capacity to do so. Each act of migration serves to confirm these relationships in that it reproduces the social relationships that determine the form and direction of the act in the first place.

A specific example of this process is available from the very considerable migration that took place from Ireland to Britain during the nineteenth century.

Irish migration to England, Wales and Scotland

The relationship between the peripheral economy of Ireland and the central core of the English economy was one which disadvantaged Ireland throughout the eighteenth and nineteenth century. Economic exploitation had been supported by political control, the transplantation of Ulster and the post-Cromwellian grants of land and property to English and Scottish settlers. Thus religious persecution following the penal laws against Catholics and political exile was part of the Irish experience from early in the eighteenth century. As Newenham stated in a book about the Irish population:

If then the trade of Ireland was so fettered, and its agriculture so confined, as not to afford employment to its population, annually increased under the operation of the causes formerly noticed, and if the existing laws were of a nature to render the greater majority of the people supremely miserable, it can afford no matter of surprise that notwithstanding the extraordinary physical advantages of that country, it was distinguished above all others by an immense emigration of people.[13]

Clearly these features outlined by Newenham represent very significant reasons for emigration but one also has to see how these initial factors develop an interrelationship that provides a context favourable to the idea of migration.

Between 1841 and 1961 the population of Ireland as a whole was almost halved as the result of migration and, despite high fertility, a combination of factors such as late marriage and low marriage rate led to a continually declining population until after the 1960s. This emigration was not new but it rose to a peak after the famine in 1846 and by the 1880s two-thirds of the people born in Ireland were living outside the country. Between 1820 and 1910 nearly five million left Ireland on the long sea routes bound for the United States, Australia and Canada. By 1891 there were 227,000 Irish-born in Australia. The passage to Britain was much shorter and with the development of steam packets after 1818 became an area of intense competition. As a result fares were much reduced and there was considerable overcrowding of the the vessels. There was no national count by birthplace in England and Wales until 1841 by which date there were 400,000 Irish-born in England, Wales and Scotland and they represented 1.8 per cent of the population of

England and Wales and 4.8 per cent of that of Scotland. By 1861 after the famine influx the Irish-born formed 3.0 per cent of the population in England and Wales and 6.7 per cent of that of Scotland, with particularly heavy concentrations of settlement in the Midlands. The immigrants went to the areas of new growth and expansion, and whereas in the 1831 Census it had been London, Manchester, Bradford and Halifax that were gaining numbers it was now Birmingham, Leeds, Bolton and Preston.

Although migration to Britain declined from a peak in 1861 it was to rise again after 1920 with extensive post-Second World War migration, especially to the large urban conurbations and the new centres of post-war industry. In the 1950s the Irish-born in Britain were a predominantly young population, 56 per cent of the females and 48 per cent of the males being aged between 20 and 39. Typically also with the late marriage age that prevailed at that time in Ireland the immigrants of both sexes were single.

These moves by the largest minority population in Britain clearly had a substantial impact, especially in areas of heavy settlement in the large cities, just as the heavy flow of migration from the south and west of Ireland left desertion and a distorted population structure in its wake.

These examples drawn from France and Ireland are only sketched here but they illustrate clearly the complexity of any consideration of why people move. Neither the moves nor the decisions that bring them about are taken in a practical vacuum. They are part of a process that has become institutionalized by previous migrations, the routes are known and very often the migrant will have relatives or friends to join on arrival. Economic links will be secured by remittances sent home and fares sent to allow younger siblings to follow. The immigrant community establishes its own churches, pubs, clubs, cafés, sporting activities and gains support from the area of origin. A complex institutional framework develops which is both supported by and itself in part supports the migration process.

The migrant is a vehicle of change encapsulating the experience of two societies; he is as much a challenge to the social milieu that fails to hold him as he is to that to which he comes. The success of the endeavour in population mobility is tested by the outcome in each case. This depends in large measure on issues related to the

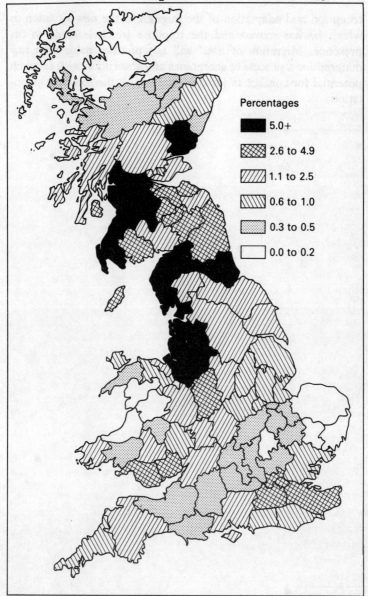

Fig. 4 Percentage of population born in Ireland in the countries of England, Scotland and Wales in 1861

Percentages

5.0+

2.6 to 4.9

1.1 to 2.5

0.6 to 1.0

0.3 to 0.5

0.0 to 0.2

reception and adaptation of the migrant to the new situation to which he has moved and the response which is made to his presence. Migration of itself will not produce more than raw material for a process of acceptance and absorption with as much potential for conflict as for conformity with the receiving population.

4
ASSIMILATION AND ACCOMMODATION

The absorption of migrants is very dependent on the policies adopted by the host society in receiving the immigrants and the attitudes of the people most immediately affected. To a lesser extent it may depend on the preparation that the migrant has received in advance and the extent of preparation and planning that has gone into the move. Policy as such will be discussed in the next chapter but it needs to be noted that official regulations or the lack of them regarding the access of migrants to receiving countries are both a product of and themselves affect the characteristics of the migration and the attitudes towards the migrants.

In this chapter and the next the emphasis is predominantly on the process of immigration into the United States and Britain and the policies developed in Britain in the post-war period. Control at national borders is more specific and easier to enforce at border points and for this reason it and the policies relating to it are more visible. Equally the effects of immigration from outside a country are likely to be more dramatic and immigrants who speak another language or dress in different ways are clearly more visible. However, it is important to bear in mind that the social process of adaptation to a new environment, accommodation to new normative and moral and cultural expectations and eventual assimilation, if it occurs, into the receiving society are the common experiences of migrants of all kinds.

The United States

Some receiving countries have had a clear policy with regard to immigrants. The United States at least until the 1930s was concerned to express the intention of a melting pot of nations whereby immigrants drawn from all over the world should become by a process of training and resocialization 100 per cent Americans. Fired by intentions of nationalism, patriotism and within the context of a functionalist model of society, the socialization of diverse strands of immigration to form an American amalgam was based on a concept of a uniform holistic model of society in which cultural dominance was assumed to be secured by the then still dominant group of White Anglo-Saxon Protestants (WASPs) who gave their mark to the country and its language.

Within this context the adaptation necessary was assumed to be principally a problem for the immigrant who must learn enough of the language, the laws and customs of the country to qualify for citizenship. Training programmes for future citizens, language classes and immigrant schools were set up for this purpose. This assimilation model assumes that each immigrant becomes a new American although it is recognized that it may take two generations to achieve this and consequently many accounts of the assimilation process attest to the conflict that developed between parents brought up in the old tradition in Europe and children reared as Americans, knowing nothing of the old country from which their parents came. By the time these children have children of their own it is assumed, from the point of view of the assimilation model, that the distinction of origin will be weakened and have no real significance within the common framework shared with other Americans.

The actual persistence of ethnic identity, particularly with those whose origins were not European, served in a practical way to minimize the effect of the myth of homogenization. Chinese and Japanese, Mexicans and Polynesians, Cuban and Arab challenged the dominance of the earlier exiles from Europe. More importantly at a conceptual level ethnicity defined a way of giving specific meaning to a distinction conferred by membership of an ethnic background. This was particularly the case when earlier 'Untermensch' groups such as the Irish, described in nineteenth century Boston as 'white niggers', gained power, wealth and status; they provided an alternative cultural framework that celebrated their roots and origins which were to be treasured and indeed preserved against the forces of secularization and conformity.

Accommodation then describes a give-and-take on the part of both the immigrant population and the resident population where there is recognition of the needs of migrants to relate to their origins and the institutions which the immigrant community has developed for its own people in religion, education and social and cultural life.

Accommodation and the concept of ethnicity which it gives rise to may generate tension and conflict around the unequal distribution of rewards in terms of jobs, housing and spending power. The ghettoization of cities with overcrowded and poor immigrants encouraged this effect and created a sharp polarization between the rich and powerful and the poor which has been reflected in the development and structuring of American ethnic experience. In many ways the experience of immigrant minority groups in the United States must be equated with the experience of the much larger black minority derived from the slave population brought to America before the Civil War. This relationship is well established by Marger[1] in an important recent text in which he accepts that we can conceptualize three types of racially or ethnically mixed society which he describes as Colonial, Corporate Pluralistic and Assimilationist. These are outlined in the table reproduced on pp. 54–5 but can usefully be given fuller discussion here.

Colonial societies

This model includes all of the slave societies and colonial settlements from the seventeenth century in which a dominant group defined and limited the actions of the minority for its own purposes. Normally the dominant group has won the land by conquest and force remains the main weapon ensuring the subjugation of the minority group. Although force is supported by law, as Elkins[2] shows with regard to the slave societies of the Southern United States, there is little redress under the law for the minority. Usually a racist ideology ensures that the subordination of the minority, the limitation of rights and the lack of social, political and economic opportunities is accepted, at least by the majority, as perfectly natural. The minority population – such as the blacks in the Southern Confederate States in America, colonial India and present-day South Africa – are kept effectively repressed. Even where a margin of equality of competition in the economic sphere is

TABLE 3 *Three types of multiethnic society*

Feature	Colonial	Corporate pluralistic	Assimilationist
Initial contact between dominant and minority groups	Conquest of indigenous groups by dominant groups or involuntary migration of minorities	Annexation or voluntary immigration	Mainly voluntary immigration but involuntary immigration and conquest for salient minorities
Relations between dominant and minority groups	Paternalistic or competitive	Ideally equalitarian, but often competitive	Competitive
Nature of stratification	Caste or castelike; caste and ethnicity overlap closely	Class hierarchy within each ethnic group	Class; class and ethnicity generally overlap, but minority group members are dispersed throughout general class system
Segregation between groups	Very rigid; explicitly defined and enforced by tradition and law	Voluntarily rigid; groups ordinarily concentrated in distinct territories	Mild and largely voluntary for groups culturally and physically similar to dominant group; rigid and involuntary for salient minorities

different... it shorter (if he still) all covers of the dominant group and is based on relative and recognition of adaptive in community. Rather it situations such as we noted; ... solution when obviously possible when ... trend creates complex.

Institutional separation among ethnic groups	High, except in economy	High, except in economy and central government	Low in polity and economy; relatively high in other areas
Physical and cultural differences between dominant and minority groups	Sharp physical differences; sharp cultural differences, at least initially	Usually slight or no physical difference; key cultural difference usually language or religion	Broad range of physical types; sharp cultural differences initially
Main objectives of ethnic policy	Inequalitarian pluralism	Equalitarian pluralism	Assimilation; some degree of unofficial structural pluralism for racially salient minorities
Degree of conflict among ethnic groups	High eventually, though usually subdued for long periods	Relatively low except on matters pertaining to cultural and political rights	Variable, but generally high between racially distinct groups
Examples	Antebellum U.S. South; colonial India; contemporary South Africa	Switzerland, Yugoslavia, USSR, N. Ireland, Canada (partially)	US, Australia, Brazil, Israel

allowed it is subject to the will and discretion of the dominant groups and is based on effective non-recognition of identity with the minority. Rather a structure such as apartheid is sought as a solution which ultimately maintains and reinforces the separation.

Corporate pluralism

In this situation there is not necessarily any single dominant group within the society. Usually in such societies there is a fairly even balance in political and social power so that no one group is disadvantaged to an extreme degree. Each group may maintain claims against other groups but a symbiotic relationship exists where each minority tends to have more to gain within the society than outside it. A good example is the situation of French Canada or that between Protestants and Catholics in Northern Ireland or Greeks and Turks in Cyprus. There tends in such societies to be constant, but scarcely resolvable conflict and tension between the two groups, each of whom claims the dominance which the existence of the other denies. These are societies within which ethnicity has greatest significance.

Assimilationist

Such societies assume that minority groups should become absorbed into the majority culture and no necessary barriers to this are seen to exist. In these situations each ethnic group can be seen to be competitive with all the others in the attempt to gain recognition but the model assumes that members of ethnic groups are not specifically excluded or disadvantaged from competition in the wider society. This competition may be somewhat unevenly achieved due to the clustering of ethnic groups at particular points in the economy or political organizations and their variable success in establishing a power base.

As Marger shows these three types correspond to three specific historical circumstances. In the colonial case groups are brought together by conquest or largely involuntary migration (as with the convicts taken to Australia). In corporate pluralistic societies groups that were previously separated as part of larger communities are brought together, often involuntarily. Thus the partitioning of Cyprus or Ireland brings about a particular balance. In both these cases there are external reference points. In the case of Cyprus the Greek and Turkish communities claim affinity with and demand recognition by Greece and Turkey respectively. In Northern Ireland as Harold Jackson shows most effectively,[3] the dominant Protestant population is only a majority so long as partition exists between Northern Ireland and the Irish Republic. In a united Ireland situation they would be a quite small minority of the total population.

The assimilationist societies are the product of relatively free voluntary migration in which there is an expectation of some degree of homogenization as the result of the migration process even though cultural and physical visibility of the immigrant minority may, for a time, make them identified as distinctive and they may consequently suffer some degree of prejudice and social exclusion which causes a degree of segregation to develop.

Although the United States in the period since the middle of the nineteenth century fits closely to the assimilationist model it is notable as indicated earlier, that there has been a fairly sharp decline in the assimilationist ideology consistent to some extent with the weakening dominance of the old stock and the increasing claims on power by other immigrant groups who could challenge the dominance of the WASPs. As Glaser and Moynihan put it 'it was important to be white, of British origin and Protestant. If one was all three, then even if one was an immigrant, one was really not an immigrant, or not for very long'.[4]

The alternative pattern which is gaining some ground is that of a vertical mosaic, a term used by Porter[5] in relation to Canadian immigration somewhat similar to the *verdeling* of the Netherlands. In this conceptualization the principle of cultural pluralism is accepted but it is also still clearly divided in terms of access to power and opportunity. Thus in Canada Porter depicts both French and British Canadians as the core dominant populations with a high degree of local and occupational specificity in the distribution of other immigrant groups.[6] The native Indian population remains at the bottom of the hierarchy.

In the United States there is clearly a hierarchy of a similar kind. Marger shows how a measure of assimilation can be used distinguishing (1) cultural assimilation, (2) access to economic, political and social institutions at all levels, and (3) equal acceptance with the primary group in relation to intermarriage, residence and access to club membership. While north-western Europeans score high on each of these components, the Irish are still somewhat excluded on the third. Southern and Eastern European Catholics, Jews, Asians, Mexicans, American Indians and Blacks all score low on the third item and only have moderate or low scores on the other two dimensions.[7]

Such an analysis demonstrates that assimilation and accommodation mechanisms are related closely to the extent to which the minority group conforms to the existing differentiation pattern within the host society. The dominant ideology defines norms that preserve the agenda of dominance and this tends to be reflected in the worldwide experience of prejudice and stereotyping of immigrant and minority populations who are described by terms intended to preserve their definition as an outgroup in a pecking order of power and competitive advantage.

The United Kingdom

The experience of accommodation to British society by immigrants over an even longer historical period is basically similar. In spite of the fact that there is enormous diversity in the origins of the English population there is still a strongly held assumption that the basic stock of Anglo-Saxon Caucasians is pure and undiluted and potentially threatened therefore by immigrant 'invaders'. The WASP mentality of the dominant ascendancy in Britain, the power elite in C. Wright Mills terms,[8] is an English rather than a British elite, even though the Englishness is made up of names and origins drawn from throughout Europe and extensively from the Celtic periphery of Wales, Ireland and Scotland.

Although contemporary debates about immigration policy and British society tend to be focussed on the race issue, the attitudes expressed by the English toward their Celtic neighbours showed a capacity for prejudice and antipathy of a high order among the English of all social classes in the nineteenth century. Particular calumny was reserved for the Irish because they were poor, rebellious and Catholic. In British cities, as Bateman writes at the beginning of the nineteenth century, they were 'crowded together with all their native habits of filth and ignorance'.[9] Again it was hardly surprising if many of the Irish immigrants brought with them to Britain the marks of a history of British oppression and violence. From the Cromwellian suppression, the rising of 1798, the Famine, the 1848 rebellion and the whole legacy of struggle for freedom from British domination that culminated in the Easter rising in 1916 the history of Ireland was part of each immigrant's luggage. Lastly, their religion distinguished them from the majority of their English neighbours, and maintained them in a tradition and faith that even English Catholics found it difficult to acknowledge as their own – in part because of allegiances with other Catholic countries that were assumed to arise from it. As Mrs Charlton wrote in a book published in 1949 recalling the end of the 19th century – 'an English Catholic not an Irish one which is all the difference in the world'.[10]

Throughout the nineteenth century the Irish were not only the most numerous immigrants in Britain but as immigrants they were perceived as a threat, they were strange, wore unusual clothes, talked with unfamiliar accents, had different habits. If anything they appeared as a most potent threat to the working class as a pool of cheap labour that could be and was in some instances, used to suppress wages.

The situation clearly varied in different parts of the country and in any case was offset by the very positive contributions that the immigrant community made to the labour movement and to political life toward the end of the century. By this time in any case the Irish community was no longer growing as fast and other settlers were appearing to focus English prejudice, particularly Russian and Polish Jews from Europe and Chinese.[11]

In all of these instances it is clear that the 'host' society did not react to immigration without the expression of a strong prejudice against the outgroup of the immigrant, a prejudice which was reinforced especially against the black immigrants of the twentieth century by the attitudes cultivated in the experience of Empire. The ideology of racial superiority and as Walvin puts it the 'divinely inspired – and justified – role in dominating and manipulating the non-white races'[12] made it difficult for the English at home to accept either the decline of imperial power or the concept of black equality in England itself. As with the Irish the repression that formed part of imperial control, the violent suppression of rebellion in Jamaica in 1865, India in 1857 as well as later struggles with peoples seeking to shake off the imperial yoke served to confirm the prejudices more strongly and the need to affirm and maintain dominance.

Migration to Britain following the Second World War was in fact made up of many groups, uprooted refugees from mainland Europe, a new wave of migrants from Ireland and increasingly immigrants from the British Caribbean, India and Pakistan. As was the case with other former colonial powers in Europe the former colonies turned to the homeland not only to provide labour needs in Europe but to fulfill promises given in the heady days of imperialism. Loyalty to a common monarch, the mother country of language and culture, education and government imposed as a model throughout the colonial possessions, the promise of independence or dominion status in the Commonwealth prepared a climate of attraction. When this was linked to the potential material gains available in the metropolitan countries it is hardly surprising that strong pressures for migration developed.

Since 1962, when the Commonwealth Immigrants Act was passed, the relatively open door offered to the citizens of the former Commonwealth began to close. The conflicting interests of trying to provide for Britain's manpower requirements; to make it possible for white settlers and their families in the former colonies to return to the 'homeland'; and at the same time to preserve a liberal stance on race relations issues, while increasingly making it difficult for coloured people to settle in Britain, suggest the climate in which policy was formulated in the period since the Second World War. This policy and its effects are considered in the next chapter.

The process of settlement

Before turning to the broader policy issues it is important to note that the common pattern for migrants is so far as possible to achieve a move from the known to the known. Earlier immigrants from the same place form a basis of contacts and communication that can assist and guide in finding jobs, accommodation, schools and social life. There is therefore a tendency for new arrivals to cluster together, with the result that significant groups of immigrants in one area give a far more pronounced impact to a migration that would be hardly noticeable if it was evenly distributed throughout the population.[13] This clustering effect has been responsible characteristically for the development of conflict and tension between the immigrant and the receiving community and has been enhanced by the fact that the immigrant was usually competing with the most disadvantaged groups in the native community. The development from this base of immigrant institutions, shops, pubs and clubs, churches and even media, served to remind the local resident that there was an 'alien presence in the midst'. The presence of these alien communities whether Irish, Jewish, Pakistani, West Indian or Chinese has significantly altered the character of Britain, its way of life and perhaps most importantly its definition of itself. The presence of ethnic diversity, racial variety and religious variety, particularly when reinforced by the native-born children and grandchildren of these migrants, makes it difficult to anticipate an outcome built around the assimilationist model. An alternative model, whether defined as a vertical mosaic or by some other pluralist concept, represents a major effect of a migration that is still small in numerical terms – the New Commonwealth Immigrants in the mid-1970s accounted for about 3.3 per cent of the total population – but large in its long-term cumulative effects.

5

MIGRATION POLICY

The control of population movement has been a natural adjunct of
the development of the nation state and the definition of a population defined by citizenship, looking to the state for protection and
available to the state as manpower for productive and military
purposes. As has already been indicated the state may intervene in
population policy by measures that ameliorate the death rate or
endeavour to influence the birth rate. Such measures, however,
tend to be long-term in their effects whereas policy directed at
migration can often have a rapid outcome. A number of examples
taken at random will indicate specific policies directed at migration
behaviour. I will list these under four headings: labour, housing,
social control, taxation.

Labour

Most generally immigration controls will specify needs for scarce
labour skills and will limit admission to migrants with such skills or
with a certain minimum of capital to let them set up their own
business. Thus Australia has modified its immigration policy in
recent years to certain classes of occupation as has Canada in
response to increasing pressure from their own nationals for some
protection in the labour market. Alternatively countries with
labour needs such as the major West European states after the
Second World War may recruit labour on a temporary basis only in
the expectation that the 'Gästarbeiter' would, after a period of
years, return to their own countries. Increasingly a coordinated
manpower policy has been developed to try to predict regional and
national needs and devise policies to satisfy them.[1]

Housing

Housing policies generally relate to relocation strategies within national boundaries, such as measures to encourage redundant coalminers to move away from uneconomic pits or the relocation of population from the East End of London in the New Towns.² They may however have international implications where a policy is developed to encourage emigration so as to relieve crowding. Certainly this was one of the number of factors written into the policy of the Netherlands government to encourage resettlement of its nationals outside Holland.³

Social control

Social control may be exercised by states both against their own citizens and against intending immigrants. Thus certain categories of persons who have committed criminal offences may be refused entry and certain possessions of migrants may be confiscated. In some instances residents of a state who have committed an offence will be exiled or bound over by the courts to leave in a modern-day equivalent of the convict ships which took substantial numbers of immigrants to Australia.⁴

Health restrictions may also be exercised in a similar way to prevent carriers of certain conditions and those who have not been immunized from crossing national boundaries. Thus immigrants are themselves given protection but also such measures prevent dislocation of health policies aimed at the native population.

Taxation

Taxation matters are largely related to the attempts made by those liable for considerable amounts of tax to relocate so as to be taxed at a less punitive rate. In general such people seek 'tax-havens' where the states concerned either have a low rate of taxation or more generally give certain exemptions to particular desired categories. Thus the Irish Republic gives a tax concession to all producers of creative works of art resident in the state. This policy initiated in the 1960s served to attract a number of significant writers and artists to live and work in Ireland. Since the exemption only applies to primary income earned directly from creative activity, the more successful have tended to leave again in recent years because an increasing amount of their income was drawn from interest on investments and accumulated capital and was therefore no longer exempt.

Ethnic and racial

Most states experience pressures that lead them to define migration policy in favour of certain groups rather than others, and much of the controversy that surrounds migration policy today in Britain relates to discrimination in terms of race or colour. Countries that practice apartheid such as South Africa specifically exclude blacks from certain areas and require them to live in certain designated townships or homelands. The United States for many years has practised a specific quota policy restricting the numbers in particular ethnic categories who might enter the United States and had local controls on residential access.

Such national policies are drawn up in response to many varied interests and intentions on the part of the legislature. In general migration policy is the consequence of an attempt to reconcile differences and contradictions of interest. Consequently it is hardly surprising that the immigration policy exercised by a country such as Britain in recent years has been subject to much controversy and appeal. In May 1985 for instance the European Court of Justice ruled against Britain with regard to allegations that the Commonwealth Immigrants Act is discriminatory.

In the post-war period all of the major European industrial nations have developed specific policies with regard to the movement of migrants across their borders. In almost every case this period has coincided with the decline of their imperial role in which they were for the most part net exporters of migrants to the colonial areas that were being developed throughout the globe. The opportunities provided in the colonial territories for labour of all kinds were gradually withdrawn as these countries achieved independence and the new nations increasingly replaced imported manpower with their own nationals. Often in the first stages of independence non-nationals or those too evidently associated with the administration of the old imperialist regime were forced to repatriate and a return migration ensued of such colonists, many of whom had in fact no ties to the homeland itself and indeed often had been born in the colonial territory.[5]

A retraction of overseas possessions and a consequent loss in labour opportunities occurred in Italy, France, Holland, Belgium, Portugal, Germany and Britain and left an often ambiguous situation with regard to the status of citizens of their former colonies. As part of the process of imperial development and incorporation, colonial peoples were encouraged to identify with the homeland and its interests. They were taught its language, honoured its royal family and responded in large measure to its laws. The educational system was modelled on that at home and assumed to be compatible with it. The administrative structure was similar to that at home and civil service and other officials expected free movement between the home and the overseas administrative structures. Identity with the homeland thus became part of the process of national incorporation on a global scale in which French, German, British or Dutch culture defined a complex sense of identity for those born in and living in their territories. Obviously this attachment varied in different sectors of the colonial populations and vied often with tribal and traditional attachments on the one hand and the commitment to new nationalist movements on the other.

This situation produced a high degree of expectation among colonial populations that they had a *right* of repatriation to the homeland. Although this expectation was greatest among those who had been born and reared in the homeland and had come out to work and 'settle' in the colonial territory, it was not limited to them but was shared by all those who either felt themselves alienated by the new regime or who could not find employment or see economic opportunity once the resources of the imperial power had been withdrawn and the independent nation was forced to depend on its own resources for economic development. This process tended in any case to bring about policies of land redistribution, labour relations, taxation and citizenship that were increasingly disadvantageous to the old-style colonial settlers.

This book is not the place to develop in detail the process of 'decolonization'. Nevertheless it set the pattern for the development of migration policies internationally during the second half of the twentieth century and led to the construction of formal measures of immigration control in all of them. Although the experience of each imperial nation and each former colony has been different, the case of Britain and its former colonial possessions can be used to illustrate the complex difficulties that surround the development of immigration control generally.

The 1962 Commonwealth Immigration Act

The 1950s were a period of rapid expansion in the British economy, including a large amount of public sector expenditure on roads, transport and housing following the end of the war and post-war reorganization. This boom situation attracted many immigrants from traditional sources such as Ireland and a large number from the West Indies, India and Pakistan. Although the numbers involved were never very great and made up no more than 3–4 per cent of the population of England and Wales the distribution of the immigrants was uneven and there were heavy concentrations in some areas. In the case of immigrants from Ireland for instance, while the Administrative County of London had a 3.3 per cent of its population Irish-born in 1951 the percentage in Paddington was 8.4 per cent and eight other boroughs had more than 5 per cent of their population who were born in Ireland. The immigrants also tended to be disproportionately young and concentrated in certain occupational sectors, with the result that within certain areas and certain employment and residential contexts they appeared more numerous. This situation led to fears that the influx of immigrants would alter, dilute or destroy traditional British forms of life. A certain degree of this fear and prejudice was directed toward the Irish who were in any case Britain's most numerically significant minority community. However, the major political pressures surrounded the coloured immigrants who represented apparently alien customs and a way of life that was not known or understood in Britain. Moreover latent racial prejudice had in some measure been reinforced by the returning ex-colonials who came back to Britain after the war. This element of racial prejudice is the key to understanding the character and the contradictions of post-war British immigration administration and it is necessary to keep it in mind in the discussion at all times. It is also important to remember that there is often a wide gap between the enactment of legislation and the operation of mechanisms for its fulfilment.

The first legislative measure in Britain to control entry of immigrants was the Aliens Act of 1905. It was directed particularly against competition from nationals of European countries, especially Jews. It thus closed the door of free entry to Britain for work or settlement and defined a distinction of major administrative importance between citizens and non-citizens. It must be noted that these were concepts of no great importance during Britain's 'open-door' period but pressures developed to distinguish between nationals and non-nationals in succeeding legislation in 1914 and 1919. The primary distinction in the legislation was between foreigners and British and the concept of British was at that time defined by the Imperial Act (1914) as including 'everyone born within the allegiance of the Crown in any part of the Empire'. It is this concept of membership of the British community under the protection of the Crown that increasingly came to be questioned after the war and in relation to significant numbers of Commonwealth immigrants exercising their rights to enter and settle in Britain itself, or any other part of the Commonwealth.

The contradictions in the matter were first addressed in 1948 in the British Nationality Act which was largely inspired by the independence of India in that year. That Act made a distinction between Commonwealth countries that had achieved independence and those which had not and were considered still to be part of the British Empire. These latter maintained in the Act full rights of entry and settlement and it was under these provisions that most of the 1950s Commonwealth immigrants entered the country.

Although the principle of open access was maintained in debates by both major political parties, the pressure for control on immigration was mounting. The apparent increase in West Indian, Indian and Pakistani immigrants during the 1950s was difficult to substantiate numerically and therefore was liable to be inflated by those pressing for either control or limitation. It was not until the results of the 1961 Census became available in 1962 that the true picture could be described. During the previous decade there had been substantial increases in immigrants from India, Pakistan, the West Indies and the Far East. It was estimated that the total 'coloured' population was now 336,000, an increase of 351 per cent on the 1951 figure of 74,500. This was made up of 81,400 Indians, 24,900 Pakistanis, 171,800 West Indians, 28,600 from the Far East and 19,800 from West Africa.

It should be noted that these figures are relatively small when set against a home population of 51,283,892. Indeed they are insignificant when compared with the one million Irish-born living in Britain, many of whom had entered Britain since the end of the

Second World War and who now constituted some 1.85 per cent of the population of England and Wales.[6] It should also be remembered that part of this post-war migration was the result of direct efforts to recruit scarce labour, not only among the Irish and other European groups such as Poles, but also in the West Indies and West Africa.

What gave political salience to the numerically small numbers of 'coloured' immigrants was a blend of racial prejudice, the evidence of their presence provided by skin colour and a range of fears and suspicions against customs and practices of dress, religion, diet and domestic arrangements that were considered strange and threatening to the 'British way of life'. The fact that they were perceived to be threatening emphasizes the extent to which insecurity and uncertainty affected Britain at this period when the initial euphoria of post-war adjustment had worn off and a certain disillusionment had set in with regard to the future of the Welfare State. A resurgence of regionalism including Little Englandism that subsequently led Britain to stay out of the European Common Market was only one factor in this process. More striking was the evidence of loss of power and position in the post-war world. This was most apparent perhaps in a perception of the loss of Empire as increasing numbers of former colonies gained independence, often only after bloody and expensive campaigns. The Suez crisis of 1956 and Britain's ultimate retreat from an exercise of old fashioned gunboat diplomacy demonstrated most clearly the degree to which the values and ideas of imperial Britain had been overtaken by the reality of a post-war realpolitik based on the power of the USA and the USSR. Although most of the old powers of Europe suffered similar retrenchments with regard to their old Empires there is little doubt that it was particularly damaging in Britain where a ruling class had remained substantially in power, perceiving Empire as an extension of their own personalities. In a very telling description of the period Walvin writes: 'the language and attitudes of imperialism continued to haunt British politics, like the imperial ghost hovering over a political wake'.[7] The same writer makes the shrewd observation that considered within the context of Britain's global decline it becomes easier to understand the degree of feeling that the issue of immigration, especially coloured immigration, aroused in the late 1950s. For a population in Britain seeing their country decline in world influence and in economic capacity it became easy and satisfying to find a scapegoat in the immigrants who themselves symbolized so many features of those changes. As Walvin writes: 'Not only were the immigrants thought by many to be the cause of Britain's problems, but politicians from both Labour and Conservative parties were damned for their failure to see or to remedy these issues by stopping immigration'.[8]

Two other aspects of the changing circumstances of Britain undoubtedly contributed to the changes in legislative procedure which developed from the 1962 Immigrants Bill. While race had become politicized in Britain with Enoch Powell emerging as an isolated but nonetheless powerful focus for the various anti-immigrant interests, it had also become highly politicized as an issue in the United States. Extensive media coverage of the Kennedy era and the Johnson aftermath heightened consciousness among Britons of the realities of a racially divided society. Britain had been notably tolerant of South Africa's policy of apartheid and was now subject to increasing political pressure by world opinion, including numerous new and black Commonwealth leaders, to condemn apartheid and isolate South Africa.

All of this background helps to explain, but not necessarily to excuse, the emergence of a confused and often contradictory series of immigration controls in the period between 1962 and 1981 to which we now turn.

The 1962 Commonwealth Immigration Act was the first in a series of legislative measures used to close the door selectively to migrants from former colonial territories that remained in the Commonwealth. Specifically the Act made a distinction between those born in Britain and with passports issued in Britain and all other Commonwealth citizens, requiring the latter group to obtain a work permit to enter Britain. Although this might appear straightforward procedurally it was full of anomalies. The right to have a British passport rather than that of a newly independent state had been available and continued to be available as part of the self-determination measures. For instance, in East Africa a considerable number of Asians elected to have British passports rather than identify with the new states that replaced Kenya, Uganda and Tanganyika. Large numbers of these people finding themselves alienated in Africa sought to enter Britain in the mid-1960s and it became increasingly apparent by 1967 that there might be many thousands of these immigrants seeking to be absorbed by Britain. Faced with this threat in 1968 legislation was enacted with extraordinary rapidity (three days through all stages of parliament) to further close the door against non-white immigrants from the Commonwealth. The act limited right of entry to UK passport holders born in the UK or with parents or grandparents born in the UK. All others were to be admitted through a strictly controlled voucher system.

This legislation met in principle the double problem faced by Britain in terms of migration from its former Empire. On the one hand there were considerable numbers of white settlers, either themselves British-born or of recent British-born stock who wished to come home, finding themselves increasingly alienated by or positively excluded by new nationalist regimes in the former colonies. On the other hand there was a continuing pressure from the native population of commonwealth countries to enter Britain. However, it was by definition discriminatory in favour of white Britons and this was further emphasized by the privileged position enjoyed by citizens of the Irish Republic, no longer even in the Commonwealth, who had continued to enjoy right of entry and full voting rights in Britain without restriction.

Further legislative measures such as the 1969 Immigration Appeals Act and the 1971 Immigration Act developed the procedure further by introducing a large range of discretionary procedures and rules for the interpretation of the Act. The 1971 Act developed the concept of patrial outlined in the 1968 Act to describe those whose parents or grandparents were born in Britain and limiting right of entry to these by a system of permits administered in part by the Department of Employment and in part by the Home Office. The increasingly complex procedure for gaining entry was clearly most difficult for those immigrants from poor and disadvantaged areas in the Third World. It was also anomalous, and this emphasized the racial character of the procedures, that right of entry without patrial status had now been extended outside the Commonwealth not merely to include the Irish but also all member states of the EEC.

This outline of the development of procedures to restrict immigration into Britain in the post-war period illustrates some of the complexities of migration policy in the modern world and the almost inevitable contradictions that arise from attempts to reconcile various competitive and conflicting interests. Most evidently in Britain there was a contradiction between a colonial policy that was relatively benign and tolerant of colonial aspirations so long as they were developed in an orderly way and the labour market needs of a post-war economy. Colonial policy was considered in isolation to instrumental matters of labour and manpower. For Britain the colonial immigrants and the Irish in the 1950s and 1960s were the equivalent of the Gästarbeiter in the rest of Europe. The matter was complicated by the extent to which they had and maintained a broader claim to Britain than simply an opportunity to work. The undeniable extent to which the whole issue opened up questions of the nature of British society itself and revealed a deep and disturbing well of racial intolerance further complicated the matter.

The outline of the legislation sets out the formal structures of restriction but says little about how these have been applied in practice. Much legislation depends on the development of interpretative practice and emergent case-law for its operation. The most difficult area of resolution concerns the status of the families of immigrants. What right has an immigrant who has obtained a work permit and a right of entry on a temporary or permanent basis to bring his or her spouse, children, parents to live with him or her? What constitutes 'family' in circumstances that embrace the very wide pattern of meanings attached to the term within the Commonwealth? Does a West Indian common-law wife constitute family? Do the children? It is useful to summarize at this stage the various categories that have been created through this web of legislation. I am following here a listing given by Moore and Wallace in their excellent study 'Slamming the Door' which gives a valuable account of the difficulties imposed through the interpretative measures governing immigration control.[9] The categories they list are:

1. UK citizens; born in the UK, or with UK parents, or one UK grandparent or five years' residence.
2. Commonwealth patrials; these are Commonwealth citizens with a UK born parent; they can enter the country freely, not be deported and may vote.
3. Commonwealth non-patrials; (a) with a UK grandparent; they

do not have the *right* to enter but are freely admitted on production of an Entry Certificate. They may be deported and can vote; (b) others; have no right of entry and are not freely admitted. They may be deported and may vote.

4. EEC Nationals; all EEC nationals (with the exception of those who have gained citizenship through ex-Dutch or ex-French colonial territories) have a right to enter Britain to work and may bring their dependents. They may not vote and subject to EEC regulations they may be deported.

5. Citizens of the Irish Republic; they have no special right to enter the UK but the UK and the Republic are treated as a Common Travel area, so citizens do enter freely to work and settle. They may be deported and they may vote.

6. Others; Non-EEC, non-Commonwealth citizens; they have no right of entry, they may not vote and they may be deported.

In addition there are some stateless persons.

Many anomalous situations are not covered by these categories and are therefore subject to supplementary procedural decision. In practice the rules give very considerable discretion to the Immigration Officers regarding the admission of those in the categories that need an Entry Certificate. Certain other categories may cause further complications when their entry provision has run out or they become, for one reason or another, reclassified. Many students studying in Britain who became overstayers found themselves in an ambiguous position, as did wives or other relatives whose status with regard to the husband with whom they came had been changed as the result of divorce or desertion. Until the 1971 Act anyone who had been admitted for a limited stay could regularize their position once they had stayed five years, since they were accepted as being ordinarily resident in the UK in spite of overstaying. Moore and Wallace summarize the position as follows:

The Immigration Act gives the Home Secretary wide powers of delegated legislation and this is translated into *Rules* which are both vague and complicated – thus giving officials an almost unprecedented degree of discretion in administering them . . . This situation bears especially heavily on coloured people because a political climate has been created which predisposes officials to operate the laws according to a very strict and restrictionist interpretation because coloured immigrants are presented as a threat to Britain.[10]

Because they have been presented as a threat, the development of the procedures of control have been threatening. Intending immigrants may be detained while inquiries are being made essentially without limitation. Since they have not been admitted to Britain they enjoy no civil liberties. It is not clear to the immigrant in advance what criteria will be used to determine admissibility. Evidence is not made available to the immigrant, and so on.

Fair administration starts with fair and uncomplicated legislative controls. But as these authors conclude:

the immigration legislation is overtly racist, it fails to provide freedom after entry and instead creates categories of citizens with different basic rights. It threatens the sanctity of the family because political considerations take precedence over humanity. At the day-to-day level the administration of the law is subject to influence by the actual or assumed political climate.[11]

In many respects the operation of the particular controls that have been developed through the immigration laws and their discretionary interpretation have been specifically racist in their effects. Dummett makes a powerful case that throughout the post-war period there has been little attempt at framing an immigration policy, relating it to emigration rates from Britain or considering it in relation to an optimum population projection. As he claims, the debates in Parliament and in the press have taken for granted a national will to exclude black people from Britain. 'Each declaration that the laws must be tightened confirms the conviction of the racially prejudiced that their prejudice is warranted and shared by the country's leaders.'[11]

This discussion of the particular context of policy issues in Britain in the post-war period is an example of the complexity of the issues involved. Other countries in varying ways reflect these contradictions and may have similar difficulties in equating aspirations of nationalist zeal with the realities of plural necessity in the highly interdependent situation of the modern world economy, labour market and population exchange.

6

MIGRATION AND SOCIAL STRUCTURE

The issues raised so far in this discussion have considered the facts
of movement, so far as the official statistics allow us to determine
them, the context of migration decisions, the act of migration itself
and the policies that relate to it as well as the consequent process of
adjustment. It has been apparent throughout this brief review that
migration lies at the heart of sociological accounts of social order
and social change; social statics and dynamics. Simmel in a famous
analysis of social groups showed how solidarity was achieved by
reference to the other, the outsider, the alien.[1] Goffman in more
recent work from an interactionist perspective makes the same
point in a series of accounts of interactions that challenge the
identity of the constructed social world.[2] To the extent to which
that social world is spatially defined, the act of migration represents a challenge to the known grounds of conformity in both the
societies that the migrant inhabits.

In this chapter I want to relate the process of migration more
closely to a sociological account of the process of social struc-
turation – how structures are formed and how they are produced.
Spatial movement is not the only kind of mobility within society
and many of the issues involved in accounts of migration can be
treated from the point of view of social mobility and its concern
with actual and potential movement within the social structure.
This field has developed models of social closure and social opportunity that conceptually relate closely to the experience of
migrants. In addition, migration has been an important factor in
stimulating social mobility.[3]

Our discussion has also revealed the multiple dimensions

involved in any sustained process of movement. Viewed even as labour power within the framework of a relatively simple labour market model the skills or lack of them that the immigrant possesses may be an important differential factor. Once a more complex model of society is admitted, the effects of movement on religion, language, culture and social behaviour are extended widely and have effects that are real but not readily determined as they spread through society horizontally and vertically. While social structures cannot be reduced to simple effects of individual actions or the motivations of individual actors they are in Weberian terms to be seen as 'arising from the continuity in time of interlocking patterns of interaction'.[4] Such a view allows, as Rex indicates, the possibility of change by intervention at strategic points but it does not allow us to ignore the reality of these structures or fail to take them seriously.

In a very good study of Jamaican immigrants in London, Foner[5] directs her interest towards the implications of status change in the lives of these immigrants. This approach allows us to separate two important components of status change; on the one hand mobility up and down the status hierarchy and on the other change in the symbolic meaning of the positional change. Although too often ignored in studies of social mobility, this is a particularly relevant factor in migration situations. Being white-collar in Jamaica may have much more significance than it does in Britain, especially when the status is overlaid with the symbolic values of being black in a white society or white in a black one.

Although this is a key observation, particularly when observable racial characteristics act so powerfully to structure relations between immigrants and 'natives' in Britain, it has consequences well beyond this. The symbolic meanings of different status dimensions are examined by Foner in a comparative perspective of the cultural significance of being old, being a woman, or having educational qualifications. The experience of each immigrant group in that respect is unique. However, she notes a very general tendency for migrant women who became employed after a move to the city to gain a freedom from many features of traditional dependency defined by their cultural background. Kenneth Little in considering migration to towns in Africa among the Xhosa shows that the movement to towns by women has considerable effects once the women are earning in limiting the control exercised by their men and the older women.[6]

A central theme for Weber also is the ways in which social closure can be used to ensure economic and other opportunities for an in-group at the expense of an out-group. The exclusive access to the means of production by property owners is one such form of social and economic closure but others may have, in market terms, considerable effects on the distribution of social benefits as well as access to the labour and housing markets.

This social closure is most apparent in the labour market because it is there that the conflict between the inner and the outer dimensions of that market are most apparent. On the one hand, the development of the Welfare State, of collective bargaining and of corporatist policies of management have secured rights for the labour movement. On the other the crisis for labour has led employers to seek supplementary sources of labour, especially to fill vacancies in dirty, arduous and inconvenient work.[7]

The responses to these contradictory expectations have been well brought out in the analysis of the use of migrant labour in post-war Europe by Castles and Kosack[8] and by other commentators in the literature. To the extent that these matters involve state intervention and policy this has reflected the inherent contradictions with a policy that on the one hand wishes to facilitate the free flow of labour and capital internationally and on the other adopts protectionist strategies in relation to both in response to domestic political pressures. Habitually the immigrant is caught between these two tendencies. Since most immigration is defined in terms of temporary, unskilled or low-skilled labour the immigrant is placed in immediate conflict with the British working class in just the areas of greatest potential sensitivity to competition and conflict where there is least achievement of rights of participation and control, least unionization and most marginality.

Lacking adequate policy instruments with regard to immigration, the new arrival in Britain who, as we have seen, may already have a suspect status with regard to residential qualification may also be open to discretionary decision-making by employers and foremen, especially those hiring casual labour at work and housing officers and social workers in the community. The question of eligibility to publicly financed housing has been an area of such discretion studied by Flett[9] in which a policy of 'just deserts' would appear to be often practised by Housing Officers in such a way that immigrants were disadvantaged by failure to give adequate consideration to the question of 'need'. This arose from an understandable morality that put a premium on such matters as the length of time on the waiting list, record of social insurance contributions and a belief that if 'too many coloureds draw Supplementary Benefits, there won't be any money left for my old age pension'.[10]

As has been shown already in the broader matter of immigration policy, these areas of discretion reflect the basic contradiction in the approach to the reception of migrants by Britain. Rex and Tomlinson show that essentially the immigrant, especially the black immigrant, is likely to find little comfort in the apparent or hidden agendas of the political parties and the broad interests they represent. As they put it:

The conservative imperialist ideology lingers on in the residual idea of a common Commonwealth citizenship, but within this common citizenship, different classes of citizens are created, each having different and unequal rights. The liberal human rights ideology leads to legislation against racial discrimination but this legislation itself is modified and weakened so as to be adapted to a variety of vested interests. Finally, the socialist ideal of the brotherhood of all working men, though it survives in the ritualistic utterances of trade unionists and labour politicians, is coupled with the belief that immigrants are political blacklegs, who will undercut the price of labour and take an unfair share of the welfare rights which have been won in the course of bitter working-class struggle.[11]

The development of race riots in British cities has similarly been interpreted from a law and order perspective that, by failing to give an adequate account of the disadvantages and differentiation of the black communities involved, the age range, sex and social circumstance of the rioters, has tacitly accepted the view portrayed by the National Front that the cause of the problem is the presence of the blacks in Britain. In quite different circumstances in the nineteenth century the Irish were thought to be the cause of the problems they found and focussed attention on in British towns. Writing about their situation some twenty years ago I wrote a passage which still covers the situation as it is experienced today:

Migration like all forms of change must involve a certain degree of risk. The whole process of personal upheaval, the breaking and making of relationships; the inadequate preparation given by one cultural background for life in another; the heartaches and keening, the fears and uncertainties which all immigrants experience 'in a strange land' are a part of the price that must be paid. So too are the social consequences of population movement – anomie, overcrowding, medical and criminal problems, maladjustment, illegitimacy and prostitution. We can gain little by blaming the immigrant for the unwanted consequences of his existence. It is clear from the experience of the nineteenth century that many of the weaknesses which the immigrants' situation exposed were weaknesses in the fabric, structure and ideology of the host society. The situation is the same today when the pressures of change represented by the immigrants in Britain of whatever race, religion or nationality exposes and threatens the weaknesses, prejudices, fears and frustrations of the British people.[12]

In conclusion it may be useful to summarize the main thrust of the argument that has been developed in this study. Both the push-pull model of migration causes and the assimilation model of migration consequence which have traditionally dominated the literature have been criticized for being both too simplistic and too much oriented to individual behaviour. It has been stressed that structural causes and effects of migration need to be given adequate weight together with a realistic assessment of the ways in which specific migrants become incorporated into different sectors of the labour markets and housing market. These locations are not equal and they influence significantly the structural effects that determine the experience that the migrant has and the opportunities that are open to him. Equally, it is likely to determine the mode of adaptation or incorporation into the receiving society. In some cases a strong ethnic identity will be developed competitively within the host society, in others there will be, as Dench[13] observed with the Maltese in London, pressures to assimilate as rapidly as possible to avoid a collective negative reputation. In yet others an attempt will be made to develop an immigrant enclave of the kind apparent in Chinese or Korean immigration to California.[14] In these circumstances, as Portes describes it: 'Minorities with the necessary resources respond to dominant capitalism with a capitalism of their own which enables successive cohorts to escape exploitation in the open labour market'.[15] It should be said that such labour markets usually involve intense exploitation nevertheless.

The effects of migration

One can follow a number of recent studies[16] in a general summary of the effects of large-scale labour migration at least as it has occurred in the industrialized societies of the West and the oil rich Arab states of the Middle East. These four effects may be more or less true of specific migrations but they remain elements to be considered in each case.

1. *Reserve army.* The availability of immigrants may exert a downward pressure on wages and the security and conditions of labour of the working class. For these reasons migration may be promoted by employers even when there is a domestic surplus of labour.

2. *Selectivity.* Migration tends to improve the health and fitness of the labour force by selection or self-selection from the younger and healthier members of the sending population, and in certain circumstances the better qualified.

   There is a good deal of debate around this issue, particularly with regard to the mental and physical health of the migrants. Some writers claim that immigrants, especially from certain origins, are particularly prone to mental illnesses such as schizophrenia or alcoholism that correlate closely with the dislocating effects of migration.[17] Others, such as Eysenck[18] claim that migration is selective of the most intelligent leaving a residual in the sending country over time.

3. *Brain-drain.* There is no doubt that, particularly where recruitment of skilled or professionally qualified manpower takes place, there are savings to the receiving country in the costs of formation and training. Similarly at retirement reverse flows to the place of origin minimize the cost to the receiving country of provision. In this context it has been argued that migration should be seen as an economic contribution by the underdeveloped and peripheral societies to the core. This has probably been overall far more significant than the concern expressed by the migration flows between industrialized countries by selected professional groups such as doctors.[19]

4. *Fragmentation of the working class.* Since most migration is of unskilled and semi-skilled workers and from under-developed peripheral regions to core receiving countries there is a strong probability that the immigrants will be perceived as an underclass and will not form solidary relations with the native working class. Ethnic and racist ideologies and prejudice

obscure common economic interests and prevent the emergence of a unified class interest.

These points, based on Portes,[20] are derived from a distinction of the United States labour market into a primary and secondary sector which is a useful model for wider application elsewhere. The primary sector corresponds to those employers that we described in Chapter 2 as having an 'internal' labour market. Immigration from these firms has specific characteristics:

1. Operates through legal channels closely related to immigration laws.
2. Employment is on the basis of ability rather than ethnic origin.
3. Immigrants generally have equal mobility chances to native workers.
4. The function of immigration is to supplement the domestic labour force.

In terms of the United States which Portes is considering, immigration to this sector included the 62,400 foreign professionals, managers and technicians and the 21,300 skilled artisans admitted as legal immigrants (1978 figures). Such immigrants characteristically compete well and adapt relatively early. Such migration is significant but inevitably has rather different parameters to that which occurs in the secondary labour market. Here Portes describes the characteristics as essentially the opposite of those in the Primary Labour Market.

1. Immigration temporary or illegal.
2. Employment on basis of ethnicity rather than skill.
3. Employment in casual, temporary work; little or no opportunity for upward mobility.
4. Immigration to this sector tends to be used to discipline the domestic labour force.

The development of immigrant enclaves, studied by Bonacich and others[21] arises as a third type of 'closed' labour market based on the immigrant community where sufficient capital exists for its development. Such a concept can be used in relation to some of the more settled immigrant neighbourhoods of Britain and the considerable development of shopkeeping and business ventures in these communities. Such an enclave necessarily tends toward isolation from the main social structure and ultimately may be divisive of the society unless adequate models of involvement can be found for the leadership of such communities.

It is clear that Britain has become in the years since the Second World War responsive to the world outside it in many respects. The development of packaged holidays and relatively cheap travel has done much to break down resistance to diversity of experience in relation to food, culture and entertainment. The diversity at home and the restless tide of movement over small and great distances that brings the world to our doorstep, in human terms has yet to be fully grasped for the new kind of society that it represents. Beijer has claimed that the greatest social benefit of international voluntary migration, though there are also social costs, is the opportunity to reduce narrow nationalism in Europe and other parts of the world.[22]

This social process of migration embodies as it always has done the human material for a major reorientation of society and a development of the possibilities of shared human talent. Unfortunately, the position of migrants has been such that they have been subject to forms of exclusion that have introduced through informal as well as formal channels the structural determinants of disadvantage and thereby reinforced these determinants for both the migrant and the indigenous population. It is here that we can return to the point at which we began this book and see the migrant not only as part of a stream or process but as a social actor with the capacity to engage in what Giddens[23] calls the dialectic of control. By this he means the capability of the weak to turn their weakness back against the powerful.

The migrant by his presence in the midst of the receiving country acts as a reflection of the values, assumptions, prejudices, hopes and fears of the indigenous population. More than this, however, the migrant by his difference, his experience of another society, opens up a window on a world of alternatives in a very immediate and direct way. His presence signifies that the world can no longer be blinkered by narrow boundaries of nationalism or race or ethnic difference. The migrant's presence denotes the interdependence of social and economic aspects that characterizes increasingly a world that is moving, however reluctantly, toward recognizing the interdependence and plurality of experience that flows from the advanced division of labour.

NOTES AND REFERENCES

Chapter 1. Migration as a social process

1. Braudel, F. (1972) *The Mediterranean and the Mediterranean World in the Age of Philip II*, 2nd edn (2 vols) 1, trans S. Reynonds, William Collins Sons/Fontana, Vol. 1 especially chapters 1 and 2.
2. Baines, D.E. (1972) 'The use of published census data in migration studies', E.A. Wrigley, *Nineteenth-century Society*, Cambridge University Press, Cambridge, pp. 311–35.
3. Ravenstein, E. G. (1885) 'The laws of migration', *Journal of the Royal Statistical Society*, **48**, 167–227 and E. G. Ravenstein, 1889, 'The laws of migration' op. cit., 52 (2) 241–301.
4. *ibid*. (1889) 286.
5. Lee, E. S. (1969) 'A theory of migration', in J. A. Jackson, *Migration*, Cambridge University Press, Cambridge, 285–6.

Chapter 2. Labour market theory and migration

1. Lind, H. (1969) 'Internal migration in Britain', in J. A. Jackson, *Migration*, Cambridge University Press, Cambridge, p. 77.
2. Blackburn, R. M., Mann, M. (1979) *The Working Class in the Labour Market*, Macmillan, London, pp. 1–34.
3. Roberts, B.S. (1981) 'Migration and industrializing economies: a comparative perspective', in J. Balan, *Why People Move*, UNESCO, Paris, pp. 17–18.
4. *ibid*., p. 21.
5. Wallerstein, I. (1974) *The Modern World System*, Academic Press, New York.
6. Petras, E. M. (1981) 'The global labor market in the modern world economy', in M. M. Kritz, C. B. Keely, S. M. Tomasi, *Global Trends in Migration*, Center for Migration Studies, New York, pp. 44–63.
7. Thomas, B. (1972) *Migration and Urban Development: a reappraisal of British and American long cycles*, Methuen, London.
8. Hechter, M. (1975) *Internal Colonialism: the celtic fringe in British national development, 1536–1966*, Routledge & Kegan Paul, London.
9. McPherson, C. B. (1966) *The Real World of Democracy*, Clarendon Press, Oxford.
10. Price, C. A., 1963, *Southern Europeans in Australia*, Oxford University Press, Melbourne, pp. 212–13.
11. A useful historical account of early Australian settlement is provided in J. M. Kitson (1972), *The British in the Antipodes*, Great Emigration Series 2, Gentry Books, London.

12. Salt, J. (1981) 'International labor migration in western Europe', in M. M. Kritz, C. C. Keely and S. M. Tomasi, *Global Trends in Migration*, Center for Migration Studies, New York, p. 142.
13. *ibid*, pp. 133–57.
14. Rose, A. M. (1969) *Migrants in Europe: problems of acceptance and adjustment*, University of Minnesota Press, Minneapolis.
15. *ibid*, p. 51.
16. Hunter, L. C., Reid, G. L. (1967) *Urban Worker Mobility*, Organization for Economic Co-operation and Development, Paris.
17. *ibid*, p. 189.
18. Jackson, J. A. (1973) Migration and social change in Europe, in B. W. Frijling, *Social Change in Europe: some demographic consequences*, E. J. Brill, Leiden, p. 72.
19. Berger, J., Mohr, J. *A Seventh Man*, Penguin, London, pp. 137–8.
20. Lind, H. (1969) *op. cit.*, p. 91.
21. Alberoni, F. (1970) Aspects of international migration related to other types of Italian migration in C.J. Jansen (ed). *Readings in the Sociology of Migration*, Pergamon, Oxford, pp. 303–5.
22. OECD (1970) *Manpower in the United Kingdom*, Organization for Economic Co-operation and Development, Paris.
23. Lind, H. (1969) *op. cit.* p. 47.

Chapter 3. Migration decisions and social change

1. A position developed by Giddens for instance in his *New Rules of Sociological Method* and in subsequent works but which owes much to Marx's famous dictum that men make their own history but not just as they please. See Giddens, A. *New Rules of Sociological Method*, Hutchinson, London, p. 160.
2. Bourdieu, P. (1977) *Outline of a Theory of Practice*, translated by R. Nice, Cambridge University Press, Cambridge, especially pp. 22–32.
3. Touraine, A. Ragozzi, O. (1961) *Ouvriers d'Origine Agricole*, Paris, pp. 7–12.
4. Taylor, R. C. (1969) 'Migration and motivation: a study of determinants and types', in J. A. Jackson (ed.), *Migration*, Cambridge University Press, Cambridge.
5. Wentholt, R. (1961) 'The characteristics of Dutch emigrants', in G. Beijer, P. P. Hofstede, R. Wentholt, *Characteristics of Overseas Migrants*, The Hague, p. 231.
6. Zelinksky, W. (1971) 'The hypothesis of mobility transition', *Geographical Review*, April, 219–49.
7. Courgeau, D. (1982) *Three Centuries of Spatial Mobility in France* (Study on the Dynamics, Evolution and Consequences of Migrations II), UNESCO, Paris.
8. *ibid.*, p. 7.
9. *ibid.*, pp. 31 and 34.
10. Hechter, M. (1975) *International Colonialism: the Celtic fringe in British national development, 1536–1966*, Routledge and Kegan Paul, London.
11. Gellner, E. (1972) 'Nationalism' in his *Thought and Change*, Weidenfeld and Nicolson, London, p. 157.
12. Hechter, M. *op. cit.* (1975) *Internal Colonialism*, Routledge and Kegan Paul, London, pp. 189–90.
13. Newenham, T. (1895) *The Population of Ireland*, London, p. 57.

Chapter 4. Assimilation and accommodation

1. Marger, M. N. (1985) *Race and Ethnic Relations*, Wadsworth Belmont, California, p. 89.
2. Elkins, S. M. (1976) *Slavery: a problem in American institutional and intellectual life*, University of Chicago Press, Chicago.
3. Jackson, H. (1971) *The two Irelands: a dual study of inter-group tensions*, Minority Rights Group, London.
4. Glazer, N., Moynihan, D. P. (1970) *Beyond the Melting Pot*, 2nd edn, MIT Press, Cambridge, Mass., p. 15.
5. Porter, J. (1968) *The Vertical Mosaic: an analysis of social class and power in Canada*, 2nd edn, University of Toronto Press, Toronto.
6. *ibid.*, p. xiii.
7. Marger, M. N. (1985) *op. cit.*, *Race and Ethnic Relations*, p. 99.
8. Mills, C. W., 1979, *The power elite*, 2nd edn, Oxford University Press, Oxford.
9. Bateman, T. (1818) *Contagious Fever*, London, p. 176.
10. Charlton, L. (ed.) (1949) *Recollections of a Northumbrian Lady*, London, p. 244.
11. Jackson, J. A. (1963) *The Irish in Britain*, Routledge & Kegan Paul, London, p. 94.
12. Walvin, J. (1984) *Passage to Britain*, Pelican, London, p. 41.
13. This can be well seen in looking at the census returns for large urban concentrations, but it is important to note that aggregate figures for migrants often conceal the distributional patterns so as to minimize the effect of concentration in certain areas.

Chapter 5. Migration policy

1. Although it is notable that migrant labour often is not considered in such policy formulations. See Jackson, J.A., 'Migration and social change in Europe', in Frijling, B. W. (1973) *Social Change in Europe*, E. J. Brill, Leiden, p. 70.
2. See Young, M., Wilmott, J. (1957) *Family and Kinship in East London*, Routledge & Kegan Paul, London.
3. A good account of the experience of early settlers in Australia is given in Kitson, J. (1972) *Great Emigrations: the British to the Antipodes*, Gentry Books, London.
4. A very evocative account of the background to such experiences is provided by Paul Scott's novel *Staying On* following the independence of India.
5. Office of Population Censuses and Surveys (1978) *1977 Demographic Review*, Her Majesty's Stationery Office, London.
6. Walvin, J. (1984) *Passage to Britain*, Pelican, London, p. 137.
7. *ibid.*, p. 137.
8. Moore, R., Wallace, T. (1975) *Slamming the Door*, Martin Robertson, London, pp. 5–6.
9. *ibid.*, p. 26.
10. *ibid.*, p. 112.
11. Dummet, M. (1984) 'Making racism respectable', *The Observer*, London, 15 July, 8.

Chapter 6. Migration and social structure

1. Simmel, G. (1950) *Conflict and the Web of Group Affiliations*, Free Press, Glencoe, translated by K. H. Wolff.

2. For instance Goffman, E. (1972) *Encounters: two studies in the sociology of interaction*, Allen Lane, London.

3. The processes involved in migration often parallel closely those of social mobility. In both cases there is a category shift and there may also be similar problems of accommodation and resocialization together with ambiguities with regard to the old and new 'societies' to which the individual belongs. It is important to note here that migration may be both cause and effect of social mobility in that much structural mobility is the result of migration and individual mobility experience whether inter- or intra-generational depends upon spatial movement. For a summary account of this literature, see Heath, A. (1981) *Social Mobility*, Fontana, London.

4. Rex, J. (1980) 'Theory of race relations – a Weberian approach', in *Sociological Theories: race and colonization*, UNESCO, Paris, p. 119.

5. Foner, N. (1978) *Jamaica Farewell: Jamaican migrants in London*, University of California Press, Berkeley and Los Angeles.

6. Little, K. (1973) *African Women in Towns: an aspect of Africa's social revolution*, Cambridge University Press, London.

7. The whole question of the theory of 'a reserve army' is relevant here, and is well summarized in works such as Doeringer, P. B., Piore, M. J. (1971) *Internal Labor Markets and Manpower Analysis*, D. C. Heath, Lexington.

8. Castles, G., Kosack, E. (1973) *Immigrant Workers and Class Structure in Western Europe*, Oxford University Press, London.

9. Flett, H. (1979) 'Bureaucracy and ethnicity', in Wallman, S. (ed.), *Ethnicity at Work*, Macmillan, London.

10. *ibid.*, p. 151.

11. Rex, J., Tomlinson, S. (1979) *Colonial Immigrants in a British City*, Routledge and Kegan Paul, London, p. 47.

12. Jackson, J.A. (1963) *The Irish in Britain*, Routledge and Kegan Paul, London, p. 70.

13. Dench, G. (1975) *Maltese in London: a case-study in the erosion of ethnic consciousness*, Routledge and Kegan Paul, London.

14. Bonacich, E., Modell, J. (1980) *The Economic Basis of Ethnic Solidarity: small business in the Japanese American community*, University of California Press, Berkeley.

15. Portes, A. (1981) 'Modes of structural incorporation and present theories of labor immigration', in Kritz, M. M., Keely C. B., Tomasi, S. M. (eds), in *Global Trends in Migration*, Center for Migration Studies, New York, p. 297.

16. See for instance: Miller, M. J. (1981) *Foreign Workers in Western Europe*, Praeger, New York; Power, J. (1979) *Migrant Workers in Western Europe and the United States*, Pergamon, Oxford; United Nations Economic Commission for Western Asia (1982) *International Migration in the Arab World* (two volumes) UNECWA, Beirut.

17. A recent discussion of this can be found in relation to immigrants from Ireland to the UK in Downing, H., Shelley, E., and Dean, G. (1981) 'First Admissions to Psychiatric Hospitals in south East England in 1976 among Immigrants from Ireland', *British Medical Journal*, Vol, 282, June 6, pp. 1831–33.

18. Eysenck, J. (1971) *Race, Intelligence and Education*, Temple Smith, London.

19. Bechhofer, F. (ed) (1969) *Population Growth and the Brain Drain*, Edinburgh University Press, Edinburgh.

20. Portes, A. (1981), 'Modes of structural incorporation'.

21. Bonacich, E., Modell, J. (1980) *The Economic Basis of Ethnic Solidarity: small business in the Japanese American community*, University of California Press, Berkeley.

22. Beijer, G. (1969) 'Modern patterns of international migratory movements', in Jackson, J. A., *Migration*, Cambridge University Press, Cambridge, p. 59.
23. Giddens, A. *New Rules of Sociological Method*, Hutchinson, London.

FURTHER READING

1

There are many publications devoted to population matters. A good general introduction is provided by Kelsall, R.K. (1979) *Population*, 4th edn, London, Longmans. Another excellent introduction to the broad principles of demography is Benjamin, B. (1968) *Demographic Analysis*, George Allen and Unwin, London. For the background of population studies and the development of demography in Britain see Glass, D. V. [ed], *Population and Social Change*, Arnold, London. On fertility issues see Hawthorn, G. (1970) *The Sociology of Fertility*, Collier Macmillan, London, and on mortality Petersen, W. (1975) *Population*, 3rd edn, Macmillan, London. On migration as a process see a recent study: Lewis, G.J. (1982) *Human Migration: a geographical perspective*, Croom Helm, London, and two earlier books of readings: Jansen, C.J. (1970) *Readings in the Sociology of Migration*, Pergamon, Oxford, and Jackson, J. A. (1969) *Migration*, Cambridge University Press, Cambridge. On internal migration specifically see Kosinski, L. A., Prothero, R. M., *People on the Move*, Methuen, London, and Boyce, A. J. (1984) *Migration and Mobility*, Taylor and Francis, London and Philadelphia, and Brown, A. A., *Internal Migration: a comparative perspective*, Academic Press, London.

2

On Britain, for an excellent account of early nineteenth century experience see Redford, A. (1926) *Labour Migration in England, 1800–1850*, Manchester University Press, Manchester. On nineteenth century Jewish immigration see Gartner, L. P. (1973) *The Jewish immigrant in England, 1870–1914*, 2nd edn, Simon Publications, London. On the Irish see Jackson, J. A. (1963) *The Irish in*

Britain, Routledge and Kegan Paul, London, and on several immigrant groups the Open University text, 1982, 'Minority experience', Open University Press, Milton Keynes, for course E354
Ethnic Minorities

On post Second World War immigrants to Britain, Patterson, S.
(1969) *Immigration and Race Relations in Britain*, Oxford Uni-
versity Press, Oxford, Glass, R. (1961) *Newcomers*, Allen and
Unwin, London; Holmes, C. [ed] (1978) *Immigrants and Minorities
in British Society*, Allen and Unwin, London; Rex, J. Tomlinson,
S. (1979) *Coloured Immigrants in a British City*, Routledge and
Kegan Paul, London. From a large number of studies of specific
ethnic groups Desai, R. (1963) *Indian Immigrants in Britain*,
Oxford University Press, Oxford, Dench, G. (1975) *Maltese in
London*, Routledge and Kegan Paul, London, Ellis, J. (1978) *West
African Families in Britain*, Routledge and Kegan Paul, London,
Khan, V. S. (1979) *Minority Families in Britain*, Macmillan,
London, Wallman, S. (1979) [ed], *Ethnicity at Work*, Macmillan,
London, Walvin, J. (1984) *Passage to Britain*, Penguin, Har-
mondsworth, Foner, J. (1978) *Jamaica Farewell*, University of
California Press, Berkeley and Los Angeles.

On the long migrations to the United States, see Glazer, M.,
Moynihan, P. (1970) *Beyond the Melting Pot*, MIT Press, Cam-
bridge, Mass., Hvidt, K. (1975) *Flight to America*, Academic
Press, New York, Fellows, M. K. (1979) *Irish Americans*, Prentice
Hall, Englewood Cliffs, N.J.

On migrant labour in Europe, Berger, J. (1975) *A Seventh Man*,
Penguin, London, gives a most vivid account in words and
pictures. One of the most detailed studies of a particular group is
Paine, S. (1974) *Exporting Workers: the Turkish case*, Cambridge
University Press, Cambridge. For a general account see Rose, A.
M. (1969) *Migrants in Europe, Minneapolis*, The University of
Minnesota Press and Castles, G., Kosack, E. (1973) *Immigrant
Workers and Class Structure in Western Europe*, Oxford University
Press, London.

Although in no way comprehensive this brief list should lead
readers to studies which relate to their particular interests.